SARS-CoV-2

Unveiling the COVID-19 Leviathan

Sofie Ostvedt

The beast that wears the crown

In its putrid frigid mask

A heart of blackened lead

Hammers down on those who ask

So none will climb the mountain

And none will see the spires

The sacred dragon hijacked

Drains away their lives

From the poem

'Sacred Dragon Hijacked'

by

Fjorgyn Mitra

Contents

Preface

It is not my intention to have you agree with what is written in this book. All that I ask is that you read with an open mind and try to understand that people have very good arguments for holding the opinions that they do concerning various issues surrounding the global COVID-19 event. Maybe you will agree with some things written here, maybe you will come to question how you came to hold your own opinions, maybe not. However, consider this: in 2014, people within OECD countries reported that the trust they held in their own governments was lower than 40%, in the USA it was less than 20% [1]. Pre-pandemic trust in news media was even lower - reported to be 29% and 28% in the USA and UK respectively [2]. This would suggest that most people should treat the information they receive from government sources and from popular media with a high degree of scepticism. You would expect such populations to seek alternative viewpoints that do not originate or rely on validation from either source. Yet, paradoxically, people seem to remain overwhelmingly compliant with, and obedient to, what the government and the press tell them about reality; including what they should believe, and how they should behave.

During 2020, most people failed to question what their media sources were telling them and allowed global and state actors to collaborate in the installation of a pseudo-dictatorial regime the likes and scale of which have never been seen before. This can be accounted for by the paralysing effects of fear, the control of information, and a relentless and repetitive propaganda campaign. What has happened is nothing short of state-sponsored terrorism. People who attempted to contest the accepted narrative have been silenced, attacked, ridiculed, and financially ruined. You may have heard nothing about these things - that is how censorship is supposed to work.

Some of the information contained in this book has been successfully prevented from reaching a broad audience. A hard regime of information control and censorship has been implemented in order to push a single acceptable narrative with the intention of cultivating the behavioural obedience of the population. Even the algorithms behind popular search results were adjusted to make much information hard to come by. YouTube, a brand owned by Alphabet Inc. (also owners of Google, Nest and Fitbit) have long-since implemented a deliberate policy of censorship by removing any content that contradicted the viewpoint of the World Health Organisation regardless of the source or veracity of the argument. Repeat offenders have had their channels removed completely. This purge has included the opinions of Nobel laureate scientists, qualified and experienced front line medical doctors, and even representations made in public legislative proceedings - so much for transparency and democracy!

Sadly, this full spectrum, totalitarian style of governance has been embraced by many who, having been blinkered by a global corporate machine that is steering both state governance and popular media, have not had the privilege of hearing the counter-arguments to the policies imposed. What is written here is an attempt to redress the balance and provide evidence that there are very good reasons for questioning what has been presented to you as indisputable truth. There are also very good reasons for questioning the integrity of those who are presenting it. The way in which perception is steered and controlled can be subtle but it is completely unacceptable to suggest that hegemonic centralised control over information is necessary for health and safety. Such control is nothing but despotism and the people who desire it are selfish, unthinking infants.

The emergency laws passed in the UK in 2020 set in place a de facto fascist police state. For example, people were physically prevented from taking their elderly relatives from care homes so they could look after them at home. Others were accosted and fined for going for a walk in the countryside. Some were beaten and dragged along the floor for not putting a piece of cloth over their mouths while trying to purchase basic food provisions. Creeping nationwide citizen surveillance and the erosion of rights of ordinary people to associate and act together to protect their interests has been ongoing for many years. However, the decision of Parliament to completely suspend democracy during the pandemic was highly unusual and should concern every free soul.

Other legislative developments have been occurring during the pandemic. Through the Police, Crime, Sentencing and Courts Bill 2021, 'disruptive' protest is set to be outlawed and stop and search powers expanded. The 'Online Safety Bill' has the potential to allow unelected government appointees to decide what information is and is not allowed to be communicated online. The potential outlets for those in disagreement with the state to have their voices heard are diminishing swiftly. As such, completing a first edition of this book was made a priority over performing countless revisions and fine editing - it may be a little raw and rough around the edges. However, it has not been crafted as a piece of art nor as light titivation but rather as an urgent call for people to stop and take account of the changes in the world that have arisen since January 2020.

Psychological research suggests that people can permanently adapt and adjust to significant changes in their life circumstances after as little as two years. Once current customs are accepted, they are likely to be followed by more. It may not be long before our world is changed forever. What we lose may be irretrievable. Some may believe this 'Great Reset' is an opportunity to 'Build Back Better' but who do you think it will be better for? If current forces of change are not stopped, the world your children and grandchildren inhabit, if they survive, may look more like hell than anything you can imagine.

The book is referenced; the bibliography appears at the end. For those unfamiliar with referencing, this means that the key points of what is discussed have their origins in scientific articles, research reports, sources of statistics, news articles and other media sources. Where you see a small number in the text in square brackets, at the end of a sentence like this [n]. There will be a corresponding entry in the bibliography at the back of the book. If a word or words appear within [square brackets] in the context of a quote, this means those words have been added to or amended within the quote, or indicate the addition of emphasis.

For those familiar with academic referencing, it is not my aim to produce references that adhere to any specific style or format but to provide references in the spirit of their intended function - so that you can find and read the sources yourself. With that said, I must stress an important point: I have noticed numerous examples of online media sources, including major titles such as the BBC and Guardian, altering stories published online so that they come to be significantly different from the original. This has sometimes been done without reference or record of any change being made, nor any explanation of why it was done. As such, it is crucial when checking online sources for yourself that you take note of the date the material was last accessed (included in the reference information) and use a web archiving tool to find the originally published material on the date stated as this may differ from what is currently available directly via the provided URL. On some occasions there may be two versions published on the same day. I recommend that you read both and note how they differ.

It would have been preferable to have had much more time refining and expanding on what is included here, much has been omitted, but I am fearful that time is a luxury that is in short supply. Winter 2021 is on the way, attempts are being made to roll out digital passports and implement a new caste system based on vaccination status. The 'fully' vaccinated are being groomed both for their booster shots and for their role in castigating and persecuting the unvaccinated outcasts. Policies that prohibit movement, enforce quarantine and solitary isolation, and mandate that people must wear face coverings, are poised to return. If people acquiesce to them again, they may never be permanently free of them.

A brief disclaimer is warranted: nothing in this book should be taken as constituting medical advice and no opinion expressed or inferred should be taken as being representative of, or supported by, any of the sources referred to.

Whatever [The Science] holds to be the truth, is truth. It is impossible to see reality except by looking through the eyes of [The Science]. That is the fact that you have got to relearn, Winston. It needs an act of self-destruction, an effort of the will.

Adapted from '1984' by George Orwell

1. Introduction

During the first days of January 2020, initial reports of a newly emerging virus appeared in news broadcasts and print media. The virus had emerged in China and there was some suggestion that there was a long incubation period before disease became apparent in the infected person. The talking heads on the news were expressing concern that the virus *might* spread. For most, this initial coverage simply merged into the background noise of global events that seeped into their subconscious awareness but raised little real concern. However, for those who could assimilate two simple facts, there was a distinct sense of foreboding. Firstly, prior to the implementation of a governmental response to the SARS-CoV-2 outbreak, hundreds of thousands of people were travelling into and out of China daily. In 2019, there were around 155 million Chinese who travelled internationally and 145 million visitors entering China from other countries [3]. This makes a rough average of just over 800 000 people entering or leaving the country daily. Clearly, a highly infectious disease that appeared to have been present within the Chinese population for several weeks before being recognised and responded to, would soon be almost everywhere in the world given this volume of travel. Inevitably, as the year progressed, the disease did indeed spread worldwide. Soon, government policies across the globe began to impact upon people's daily activities, restricting freedoms and imposing systems of control and coercion which have never been seen in modern times. Most of these were adopted following advice and predictions issued by a small group of people attached to, or associated with, specific scientific and medical organisations, corporations, or funding groups. Affiliates of these organisations adopted and promoted policies of information control as rehearsed in a pandemic preparedness exercise that took place in October 2019 [456]. The name of the exercise was 'Event 201'. A name that coincidentally refers to year 20, month 1 – January, 2020 – when the SARS-CoV-2 virus began to spread across the globe.

2. The Origin of SARS-CoV-2

Where the virus came from is crucial to understanding how to manage such threats in the future. If it emerged as a result of experimentation, we may wish to consider how wise it is for such research to continue given that the full consequences of SARS-CoV-2 and the way it has been managed may, in the long-term, be more damaging than a world war. It may even lead to one. If science has lost its wisdom, its ethics, and its foresight, maybe it needs to be subdued and reigned in? Studying the discussion about the origin of the virus is fascinating. The zeal with which the initially preferred story was presented, that the virus had a zoonotic (animal) origin and it spread via a wet market in Wuhan, is intriguing by the way media channels and governments assumed this narrative and ensured it eclipsed all others. However, it was not long after the outbreak of the virus before information began to emerge that suggested the wet market narrative was problematic.

Firstly, Wuhan, the alleged source of the outbreak, was home to the Wuhan Institute of Virology - a research laboratory that had been studying how to manipulate viruses, including splicing viruses together to create more dangerous chimeras; work known as 'gain of function'. Gain of function research aims to find ways in which a virus can become more

8

transmissible, more evasive to immune function, and ultimately, more likely to cause a deadly epidemic or pandemic. Furthermore, the Wuhan laboratory was known to have collaborated in gain of function research on corona viruses; the results of some of their work had been published [4]. In 2017, an article in Nature explained that the Wuhan lab was due an imminent upgrade to biosecurity level 4 [5]. This was a matter of international pride for the Chinese and researchers suggested they were hoping to work with Ebola and the virus that caused SARS (even though work on corona viruses had actually already been carried out under biosecurity level 3). However, the article also stated that critics were extremely concerned over safety, especially considering that SARS had escaped from another Chinese research lab in Beijing on more than one occasion. These concerns were not unfounded. According to one journalist, inspections by American officials had flagged up the Wuhan Institute as operating with an unsafe approach to biosecurity in 2018, just one year after it had commenced operations at biosecurity level 4 [6].

Even based on these facts, anybody with an iota of integrity would surely suspect that the wet market story smelled a little fishy. Which begs the question as to how even the mere suggestion of a link between the virology lab and the SARS-CoV-2 virus was attacked so vehemently and consistently by popular media sources and scientists who appeared to have appointed themselves as authoritarian guardians and keepers of truth. These were the first obvious signs of how key figures in the scientific establishment would work with popular media to shape and control public perceptions over the coming months and years. 'The Science' began to emerge as a neo-Orwellian concept on a par with 'The Party' from the novel '1984' by Eric Arthur Blair, published under his pen name - George Orwell. What made the articles about the origin of the virus so conspicuous was both their certitude at such an early stage and the narrative use of dog-whistle terms like 'disinformation', 'misinformation', 'conspiracy theory', 'tin-foil hats' and 'debunked'. All terms emanating from the lexicon of western media propaganda; weaponised words used to shepherd and direct minds away from contemplating non-mainstream narratives using derision and shaming. This is not journalism but social engineering; it is bullying not reasoning. Perhaps, in this instance, there were other motives at work: an attempt to prevent an international dispute with China that could quickly escalate to global conflagration; a desire to minimise the risk of racist attacks against people of Asian or Chinese origin; or simply a knee-jerk defensive reaction by those in fear that their profession - the source of their income, prestige and influence - might come under political attack due to public pressure.

Prominent private and state media corporations maintained the policy to portray any consideration of the potential link between the appearance of a novel, highly infectious, deadly virus and a laboratory that had specifically been studying how to make this type of virus more deadly and that was located just a few miles away, as foolish [7, 8]. Some of this narrative was written by people such as Peter Daszak who, unknown to many of his readers, had considerable personal, professional, and financial conflicts of interest when it came to the issue of safety in viral research, including direct links to the work conducted at the Wuhan laboratory [9]. Daszak, who was particularly fond of deploying the phrase 'conspiracy theory', was recused from the Lancet's COVID-19 commission in June of 2021, owing to his failure to be open and honest about declaring his own significant conflicts of interest [10]. It is a shame the journal did not appear to perform due diligence when appointing Daszak in the first instance. The question is why?

The campaign of censorship and restriction of debate did not just affect discussion over the origins of the virus. By November of 2020, tyrannical control over information flows and attack-dog suppression of scientific debate led British Medical Journal executive editor, Kamran Abbassi, to state [11]:

Science is being suppressed for political and financial gain. Covid-19 has unleashed state corruption on a grand scale...

As time passed, suspicions of a laboratory origin proved not to be as outlandish or irrational as the initial propaganda campaign had made them out to be. In spring of 2021, Facebook revised its policy of censorship based on its 'Community Guidelines' allowing talk about the possibility of a laboratory origin; previous policy had been to banish all mention of this - a tacit admission of how irrational, unscientific, and authoritarian their censorship policy was in the first instance [12]. What had been obliterated under the label of irrational disinformation suddenly became possible and acceptable for debate. Had reality changed? No, but the corporation-sanctioned perception of reality had certainly altered for people who relied on the Facebook corporation to control the validity of the ideas they were exposed to. Far from a thirst for the truth, the most likely reason for this reversal of corporate policy was the increasing danger that substantial numbers of people would become aware of how throttled and controlled their information flows were when they came across compelling reasons for suspecting a laboratory origin of the virus. If they realised the extent to which dogmatic propaganda and censorship were being used to shape their understanding, they may then also come to question what other information has been kept from their purview, who is keeping it from them, and why.

Facebook's policy U-turn was justified based on 'new' information. Yet, most pertinent evidence about the potential of a lab origin for the virus was not new and exactly the sort of information they themselves had been blocking from their own platform. Very early after its emergence, properties of the virus were identified that placed significant question marks over the idea that the virus could have been the product of natural evolution. In January 2020, a group of scientists raised serious questions about structure of the virus. They highlighted the unusual characteristics of SARS-CoV-2, including similarities of the spike protein to HIV [13]. However, this paper - a preview which had not yet been peer-reviewed - was hastily withdrawn by the authors after pressure from some quarters of the scientific community.

Curiously, the link with HIV was raised again when an Australian COVID-19 vaccine manufacturer found that those inoculated began to test positive for HIV [14]. There was no suggestion the vaccine caused HIV but there did appear to be some genetic similarity between key components of SARS-CoV-2 and HIV. Either that or the HIV testing kit being used was seriously flawed. The firm manufacturing the vaccine in question decided troubleshooting the issue would be too time-consuming, and that they would be unable to find a solution within the short timeframe required to meet urgent demand for COVID-19 vaccines. Production was halted. The evidence for unusual links between COVID-19 and HIV are still largely unaddressed, but it seems that any direct links between HIV and SARS-

CoV-2 had been dispelled. By contrast, the potential for a laboratory origin remained a hotly debated topic.

In March 2020, a letter of opinion appeared in Nature suggesting that a laboratory origin seemed unlikely but did accept that this conclusion should be revised upon consideration of further evidence [15]. Around the same time, Chinese officials were claiming that the USA had brought the infection into China following its escape from Fort Detrick - a US bioweapons research site that, coincidentally, had been shut down in August 2019 due to lapses in the maintenance of biosecurity [16]. The Chinese suggested that the virus had been circulating in the USA in 2019 but its presence had been ignored or covered up. By April of 2020, UK government ministers were also considering the possibility that SARS-CoV-2 had leaked from a laboratory [17]. Shortly afterwards, French scientist Luc Montagnier (a Nobel laureate) was said to have suggested that the structure of SARS-CoV-2, including some notable similarities to HIV, pointed to a lab origin; he also highlighted the nature of the work that the Wuhan research lab had previously undertaken with corona viruses in support of that possibility [18, 5]. By June of 2020, the former head of MI6 - Sir Richard Dearlove - was quoted as saying, '*I do think that this started as an accident*' and was broaching the issue of reparations by the responsible party [19]. Dearlove's sentiments were mirrored by David Asher, a former lead investigator for the US State Department, who suggested SARS-CoV-2 could be '*a weapons vector gone awry*.' [20].

Later in the year, Yan Li-Meng - a Chinese virologist who had prior experience working in the Wuhan laboratory, produced a well-referenced paper claiming not only that SARS-CoV-2 was a lab creation but also a bioweapon that had been deliberately released by the Chinese Communist Party [21]. She pulled no punches in drawing attention to widespread fraud within the scientific community. Ulterior political motives cannot be dismissed for any of the narratives presented but in Yan's case taking on the Chinese government is an incredibly dangerous thing to do (as it would be with most national governments just ask Julian Assange or Edward Snowdon). It is notable that Yan fled China to the USA shortly after her initial revelation with support from The Rule of Law Foundation. However, they later withdrew support for her following a deterioration in her mental state which led to a deep paranoia about potential threats of assassination from perceived friendly sources. Whether justified or not, such paranoia sounds understandable given the circumstances. Withdrawing support for someone in their direst time of need seems like an odd policy.

Critics have suggested that some of Yan's claims are unsubstantiated. Remember, we are dealing with state secrets and matters of national security involving the most controlling government in the world who have deployed the most ubiquitous citizen surveillance program ever created. Focusing on the arguments presented, Yan's case is very compelling. Scientific analysis suggested that the virus had a structure with qualities that are highly unlikely to have occurred naturally. Notably, the virus appeared to have been designed to be especially transmissible between, and virulent to, humans. Additionally, links to the Wuhan wet market were said to be weak with no corroborating evidence that initial infections, nor patient zero, originated there.

In December 2020, a further report said that Chinese officials could find no evidence of an animal origin for the virus [22]. During 2020, it appeared that political tension was increasing between the USA and China. Over the summer, two US aircraft carriers were deployed to the South China Sea [23]. However, there was also an important and interesting link between the US and the Wuhan laboratory. In 2015, Dr Anthony Fauci - director of the National Institute of Allergy and Infectious Diseases in the USA, had been appointed to oversee a five-year research project based in Wuhan that involved working on corona virus in bats. His involvement included management of grants worth $7.4 million, some of which vicariously funded research that took place in the Wuhan laboratory [24].

The intrigue concerning the origins of the virus is complex. It is further confounded by confusion as to exactly when, and where, the virus emerged. The dominant story initially propagated was that the virus emerged in Wuhan, China, toward the end of December in 2019, hence this is what shaped public understanding. However, other reports present facts that conflict with this account. Firstly, there was the claim that the first case occurred in Hubei province and could be traced back as far as 17th November 2019 [25]. The possibility that the virus could have been in the UK as early as late November 2019 was also considered scientifically credible [26]. Traces of SARS-CoV-2 specific antibodies were found in blood donated in the USA as early as 13th December 2019 and confirmation of the presence of SARS-CoV-2 specific antibodies in samples that were taken in early January 2020 mean that the virus must have been present in the USA at least as early as mid-December 2019 (this is because the antibodies are said to take 14 days from infection before they are reliably detectable) [27, 28].

Elsewhere, Italian scientists claimed they found a match for the virus in a sample taken on the 5th of December 2019 from a young boy suffering with measles [29]. Another group of researchers found a small number of blood samples taken in Italy in October 2019 tested positive for SARS-CoV-2 antibodies [30]. They verified this using two different methods and suggested it was plausible that the disease was circulating at that point; the other possibility being that antibody tests are not reliable [31]. In Brazil, sewage samples taken in November 2019 were reported to have tested positive for SARS-CoV-2 [32]. Spanish scientists even claimed to have found confirmation of the presence of SARS-CoV-2 in frozen sewage samples taken in Barcelona in March of 2019 [33]. These events suggest that either there are grounds for scepticism over the original official tale of how the virus emerged from animals or that there are reasons to doubt the accuracy and efficacy of the methods being used to detect and identify the virus; perhaps both.

The WHO attempted to instigate an investigation by sending a team of experts to Wuhan but for an entire year they did not set foot in China [34]. On the 14 January 2021, they were allowed to begin the performance of their inspection. Less than a week later, and with access to crucial data denied, they declared they were unable to find any evidence for a laboratory escape [35, 36]. Despite this, they offered little information about the true origins of the virus. In June 2021, former MI6 chief Richard Dearlove, pointed out the painfully obvious - that China would have long eradicated any evidence of a laboratory origin [37]. Imagine a police investigation of a murder scene limited to take place over a few days, delayed for a year, while the suspect, still an occupant at the crime scene, had full knowledge of their suspicions, intended arrival, and retained the ability to completely block access to documents or other information during any investigation that did take place. How likely is it that such an investigation would reveal meaningful evidence? Following the token performance of the WHO inspection, the BBC reported that [36]:

Experts believe the virus is likely to have originated in animals, before spreading to humans, but they are not sure how.

In view of the lack of evidence to support this theory, and plenty to the contrary, it seems that 'believe' was the operative word. If they were 'not sure how', where is the evidence for holding such a belief? Jamie Metzl, a member of the WHO advisory committee, was later reported to have confessed that overwhelming circumstantial evidence made the idea that SARS-CoV-2 may have originated in the Wuhan laboratory far more plausible than it being a wholly zoonotic virus spread from bats [38]. Even Dr Rochelle Walinsky, a director at the US Centers for Disease Control, conceded that a lab origin was a possibility [39]. A Bayesian analysis conducted by Dr Steven Quay concluded that the probability of the virus being man-made was 99.8% versus a 0.2% chance of a zoonotic origin [40]. One of the founders of Moderna, microbiologist Derrick Rossi, also believed that the virus accidentally escaped from the Wuhan laboratory [41]. Evidence that live bats had been kept at the Wuhan lab proved that members of the commentariat, such as Peter Daszak, had not only been dishonest about their interests but also in their representations; it also meant that technical biological arguments for a zoonotic origin do not prove that that the virus could not have leaked from an animal in the laboratory [42].

Plenty of scientists outside China knew about the use of live bats - it was hardly a Chinese state secret — Australian universities had even collaborated on some of the research projects [43]. In 2021, further evidence emerged showing that there were no bats (or pangolins) traded at the Wuhan wet market between May 2017 and November 2019 [44]. Despite mounting evidence, many continued to cling to the original story - that the disease emerged following zoonotic transmission via animals sold in the market. Some people will stick to their beliefs regardless of conflicting evidence. It is a hard-wired evolutionary adaptation to ensure that one's reasoning is socially compliant [45]. In other words, to benefit one's survival it is more efficient to change one's reasoning to fit perceptions of what is acceptable than to face becoming an outcast from the group. At least it is in the short term. Those who have the most comfortable existence and/or who benefit most from existing narratives are the least likely to buck this trend. For most, short-term self-interest will trump acceptance of a difficult truth every time.

3. Testing

The declaration of the COVID-19 pandemic was directly connected to testing regimes that were implemented internationally, mostly following the guidance of the WHO. The predominant test used, particularly in the early stages of the pandemic, was the RT qPCR test (reverse transcription quantitative polymerase chain reaction). This test uses methods that find fragments of viral RNA and then artificially replicates the number of these fragments in repeated cycles until there are sufficient for the test to confirm detection. The WHO issued guidelines for performing tests based on a scientific publication from January 2020 (referred to as the Corman-Drosten paper); it had suggested a protocol for identifying cases of COVID-19 via PCR test [46]. PCR testing was soon rolled out across the globe. However, serious concerns were identified with the Corman-Drosten paper. In December 2020, an independent group of scientists published a formal request for the paper to be withdrawn [47]. Their concerns included that: the paper was published within a day of having been submitted, suggesting that a proper peer review process had not taken place; the paper was published in a journal of which two of its authors were also members of the editorial board; the proposed test suggested identification of only two genes rather than three - the latter being standard in use of PCR to *aid* diagnosis of viral disease; the methods recommended a notably high concentration of primer which could lead to a high false positive rate; the researchers developed their protocol using a computer-modelled viral genome without testing for reliability and accuracy against a real viral sample verified at molecular level; no cycle threshold was proposed, but it appears the authors used 45 - an extremely high and unreliable number unsuited to the use of PCR as a diagnostic aid. A more detailed discussion of cycle thresholds will follow later in this chapter.

Even disregarding the many issues specific to the Corman-Drosten paper, the PCR test is not reliable for disease diagnosis as a standalone measure because it only detects viral fragments and not the whole virus. This means that a positive test alone cannot determine whether a person is, or has been, infected, nor whether they are infectious to others. For reliable diagnoses, there must be an accompanying clinical diagnosis of symptoms, exclusion of other causal factors, and preferably additional supportive tests such as full gene sequencing, antibody tests etc. The need for clinical information to be used in diagnosis was explicitly stated by Public Health England [48]:

> *A single Ct value in the absence of clinical context cannot be relied upon for decision making about a person's infectivity.*

And the World Health Organisation [49]:

> *Most PCR assays are indicated as an aid for diagnosis, therefore, health care providers must consider any result in combination with timing of sampling, specimen type, assay specifics, clinical observations, patient history, confirmed status of any contacts, and epidemiological information.*

Despite this, across the globe, cases of COVID-19 were being based on a single positive PCR test [50]. This was distinctly unusual - none of the testing regimes for SARS-CoV-1, Zika virus, Ebola, H1N1 influenza, and MERS-CoV abandoned the need for additional considerations to support a positive test before a 'case' was confirmed [50]. Ideally, for definite confirmation of disease-causing infection, a viral culture taken from a symptomatic person is the only truly reliable test. This was pointed out in a letter published in March 2020 in the New England Medical Journal. The author discussed concerns about patients who appeared to test positive long after remission of any symptomatic disease and went on to highlight the fact that a PCR test alone was not adequate for proof of infectivity [51]:

> *...the viability of 2019-nCoV detected on qRT-PCR in this patient remains to be proved by means of viral culture.*

The distinction between whether a person is infectious or not is extremely important. Generally, if a person is shedding particles of virus that pose more than a very remote risk of infecting others (i.e., large numbers of whole and viable virus as opposed to broken down 'dead' viral pieces) they will be symptomatic - typically any combination of the following: runny nose, cough, sneezing, or sweating. It may be possible to find examples of transmission just prior to the onset of symptoms - what the CDC had referred to as pre-symptomatic, but this is different to asymptomatic where no symptoms are experienced at any time [52]. Unfortunately, this important difference has largely been misrepresented by scientific authors, key broadcasters, media channels, and the CDC itself who have misinformed the public about the lack of evidence showing any significant risk of spread from people who *never* develop symptoms. A study based on a sample population of 10 million people in China confirmed this - the authors stated [53]:

> *The detection rate of asymptomatic positive cases was very low, and there was **no evidence of transmission from asymptomatic positive persons** to traced close contacts* [emphasis added].

Any protocol for using PCR to help with disease diagnosis will use a cycle threshold. That is, the number of times a sample can be amplified before a test becomes unreliable; it is at, or before, this threshold that a test will be declared positive or negative. Research has shown that it becomes impossible to culture live virus from samples which test positive at cycle thresholds above 33; the most reliable results coming from use of cycle thresholds of 17 or less [54]. The levels of reliability can vary according to factors that may differ between laboratories during the implementation of their tests. Such variables include the nature of reagents used, the type and length of RNA sequences being detected, and the number of genes being tested for. However, there are two key points to note about PCR tests in general. Firstly, the more cycles required to find a positive result, the less reliable they are. Secondly, they cannot, and should not, be used in isolation of clinical symptoms to diagnose disease. Where symptoms are present, clinical investigations should be carried out to exclude other possible causes for those symptoms. This is hugely important when contemplating whether there is justification for severe containment measures that deprive people of their basic human rights. The conclusion of a review published in the journal 'Clinical Infectious Diseases', stated [55]:

A binary Yes/No approach to the interpretation [of] RT-PCR unvalidated against viral culture will result in false positives with possible segregation of large numbers of people who are no longer infectious and hence not a threat to public health.

In late spring of 2021, the Swedish Public Health Agency (SPHA) concluded that PCR tests were not suitable for determining whether somebody is contagious or not [56]. It is unclear what took them so long, or why others didn't follow suit. The reason the SPHA gave for their decision was that PCR could detect residual viral particles weeks and possibly months after infection and at a time when people were clearly not presenting any risk of contagion to others. In 2020, a meta-analysis of studies evaluating the accuracy of PCR test results used in viral infection detection suggested a median false positive rate of 2.3%, the most accurate testing regime produced a false positive rate of 0.3%. So, if you tested 1000 people with the highest level of accuracy you would get 3 positive results even when there is no disease in the sample population at all. If you tested 100 000 people per day for a year your cumulative number of false cases based on a single positive test would be over 10 000. At a false positive rate of 2.3% you would end the year with a cumulative total of 839 500 cases that were not cases at all. If all these people were quarantined for 14 days, there would be a

20

total quarantine time of over 32 000 years. That is 32 millennia of loss of freedom imposed on people neither infected nor infectious.

False positive rates can be reduced by lowering the cycle threshold used in the PCR test. Alarmingly, it is very difficult to discover what cycle thresholds were being used to support the case numbers that justified draconian limits on civil liberties and travel across the globe. There was no internationally agreed standard and the WHO advised test centres to follow test-kit manufacturer's guidelines. In the UK, Professor Martin Neil discovered that two laboratories, both run by the same firm, were not following manufacturer's instructions which required that a minimum of two genes were tested for. Professor Neil had a letter published in the BMJ which stated [57]:

> *...the UK lighthouse laboratories appear not to be in strict conformance with the WHO emergency use assessment and the manufacturer instructions for use. Given this it is clear the ONS and the UK lighthouse laboratories needs to publicly clarify their use of, and justify the reasons for, deviating from these standards.*

In the UK, a freedom of information request was submitted to the ONS in an attempt to discover data on cycle thresholds but it was rejected. The reason the ONS gave was highly dubious - that statistics on cycle thresholds could be used to identify test subjects and as such the data was considered non-disclosable personal data [58]. Surely a dataset could have been provided that contained laboratory information, cycle thresholds and corresponding decisions on positive or negative results without any personally identifiable data being included? In August of 2020, the New York Times reported that most cycle thresholds in the US were being set at 40, noting that this would produce a case detection rate tenfold higher than if cycle thresholds were set at a more reliable figure of 30 [59].

In the USA, the CDC encouraged submission of samples that had tested positive for SARS-CoV-2 so that they could be genetically sequenced. However, their guidance required that only samples that tested positive at cycle thresholds of 28 or lower should be submitted [60]. The reason being - it is virtually impossible to sequence whole virus from samples which tested positive at higher cycle thresholds because they would have no viable virus present. An article in the 'Journal of Infection' analysed a broad sample of PCR test data and found that increasing the cycle threshold from a maximum of 24 to a maximum of 29 generally produced a 50-100% increase in positive test results [61]. The authors noted that an approximately corresponding proportion of positive test subjects (45-68%) in the UK reported that they were symptom free. The authors concluded:

> *In light of our findings that more than half of individuals with positive PCR test results are unlikely to have been infectious, RT-PCR test positivity should not be taken as an accurate measure of infectious SARS-CoV-2 incidence.*

This is a crucial point. If the test cannot be considered accurate it should not be used to frighten people, remove their rights and freedoms, deprive them of contact with friends and family, or leave them out of pocket. Yet official guidance did not seem to treat the fundamental rights of the citizenry with respect. For example, Public Health England did not recommend any threshold but suggested a maximum of 40 was standard practice - as such this may well have been a figure that laboratories adopted [48]. In January 2021, as vaccine programs were rolled out globally, the WHO issued a notice of guidance seemingly as a stern reminder that laboratories administering PCR tests should be wary of using high cycle thresholds to produce positive cases and reminded them to pay close attention to the 'instructions for use' when performing such tests [49]. It is not clear what prompted this notice to be issued at this time, but it is not unreasonable to suggest that the organisation had become aware that laboratories were not following best practice guidelines (as per Lighthouse laboratories in the UK mentioned previously). Neither is it clear whether issuance of this notice had any influence on testing regimes and reported case numbers in the weeks and months that followed.

It would be extremely important to know if laboratories tightened standards for testing, and when, as this could have significantly reduced case numbers and positively influenced assessment of the efficacy of vaccine programs. Attempts to locate large data sets showing the PCR cycle thresholds used by laboratories, regions, or nations over the course of the pandemic has not yielded results. Yet, such data would be essential for use in analysis of how testing regimes were affecting 'case' counts for COVID-19, and whether techniques between nations and regions were different or had changed over time.

In epidemiology, a 'case' is supposed to be a person who is confirmed as suffering from a disease or condition. Counting cases requires a list of specific criterion which must be met. Globally, for COVID-19, there was no standard definition of a case. It appears many countries have counted cases as positive tests ignoring the need for additional criterion to be met, i.e., clinical diagnosis. For a person to be diagnosed as a 'case', and hence at some point infectious, they would require the minimum of a positive test (at a cycle threshold of 33 or preferably much lower) *and,* at the very least, they should be found positive for distinctive clinical signs upon medical examination. Yet no such scientific rigour appears to have been applied. Indeed, different countries were using divergent, and often equally spurious, measures for defining a case. For example, in the UK, a person could be tested three times, found negative on two of those occasions, be completely clear of any clinical symptoms and yet still be counted as a 'case'; in France any untested person with a symptom similar to the flu or a common cold could potentially qualify as a 'case' even in the absence of a test [62].

Another highly problematic situation is the impact of false positive results in areas of low prevalence of infection. In these circumstances, the significance of the false results could have a huge impact. Researchers have investigated this issue. One study sampled a population of over 5000 and found just 31 positive tests [63]. The tests were deliberately performed using cycle thresholds of 35 or above - noted to be of low reliability. The samples producing positive tests were then subject to further scrutiny. Of the 31 samples that had tested positive, 26 were found to have tested positive for only one gene, 3 were positive for two genes, and 2 were positive for three genes. Additionally, only 12 out of the 26 people who had tested positive for any gene showed any symptoms. Most of the 12 symptomatic participants did not have their symptoms attributed to COVID-19 by the researchers because they failed to test positive for more than one gene. The researchers argued that if the presence of multiple genes is not detected then this is evidence that there is a lack of complete and viable virus present. They concluded that only 16% of the positive tests could be reliably counted as positive indicators of infection. The remaining 84% being false. The authors of this research expressed serious concern about the many detrimental effects that could arise as the result of policies based on a great number of false positive cases. Such detrimental effects included: delayed or cancelled treatment for patients, some of whom were suffering from cancer or in need of organ transplants; short staffing caused by policies which require non-infectious asymptomatic staff to isolate at home; patients due for discharge being held in hospital unnecessarily; and additional costs from activity arising from retesting and track and trace policies. The science proving that PCR testing was unreliable was central to a legal case brought in Portugal. There, senior judges supported the decision of a lower court who had ruled that the results of a PCR test alone cannot stand as justification for enforcing the quarantine of foreign nationals and such action was in violation of both domestic and international law [64]. The case was not reported by any major media outlets.

Contentious issues with PCR testing were not limited to cycle thresholds and its misuse as a diagnostic. For example, in the USA, a scandal emerged over contamination. When the initial CDC testing regime was rolled out in March of 2020, only testing kits authorised and issued by the CDC itself were permitted for use. However, after just two weeks of use these tests were flagged as being extremely unreliable. The problem was only discovered after 24 public health test centres conducted trial tests on unused kits and found that they produced positive results [65]. A brief investigation concluded that due to rushed production the kits had probably become contaminated by exposure to reagent material and the CDC had failed to adhere to standard quality control measures which should have been in place to detect such an issue. It is not clear what reagent was said to have caused the contamination, nor exactly how it came into contact with so many test kit components.

Problems also occurred on the opposite side of the Atlantic. In the summer of 2020, the UK government recalled 750 000 tests due to undisclosed safety concerns [66]. Later that year, undercover filming revealed poor practice in testing laboratories which would undoubtedly have caused contamination and false positive test results [67]. One of the most shocking incidents reported in the UK occurred when Birmingham council was found to have

24

been handing out tests that other people had already used. This occurred during a doorstep campaign that pressured people to complete their tests ready for collection 15 minutes later [68]. This mistake was only discovered when a student noticed the swab they had been given had clear signs of prior use and raised the alarm.

Unreliability in testing regimes may also be connected with the outside possibility that sections of corona virus are being reverse transcribed into human chromosomes. To date, there is no evidence that this has definitely occurred (is anyone looking?) but laboratory research has provided evidence that it is feasible [69]; one of the potential implications for affected people is that they may test positive for the virus for a long time after an initial infection. A type of enzyme called reverse transcriptase is involved in the process of taking RNA and inserting it into DNA. Human cells produce reverse transcriptase endogenously and it is understood to play a crucial role in the maintenance of chromosomes (structurally organised DNA) [70]. Similarities have been drawn between this mechanism and the way in which retroviruses such as HIV and hepatitis B operate. However, retroviruses typically carry their own reverse transcriptase to facilitate the insertion of their RNA into our DNA. It is notable that there have been reports of people testing positive over prolonged periods of time. One example comes from Italy where a case report documented an incidence of a recovered patient who tested positive more than two months after full recovery from a corona virus infection [71]; there was no evidence of reinfection or clinical disease. The case could be explained by reliance on PCR testing regimes that use cycle thresholds of 45, in accordance with WHO guidance, and consequently detect viral fragments and not in-tact viable, infectious, virus [72].

A thorough review of testing protocols and standards, written by Dr Sin Hang Lee of Milford Molecular Diagnostics Laboratory, also noted another serious issue with testing guidance issued in the USA. The CDC had published testing protocols that only recommended detection of 25 contiguous base pairs of DNA falling remarkably short of the 100 continuous base pairs recommended by the FDA for the detection of viral disease infections [73]. (Note: the SARS-CoV-2 virus is an RNA virus and as such has no paired bases but DNA with base pairs is created from the RNA as part of the PCR testing technique.) The crux of Dr Lee's analysis was to highlight how problematic unreliable testing protocols could be. Of concern was the fact that a false positive test could condemn a person, possibly an uninfected hospital patient or care home resident, to prolonged containment in quarantine facilities, or on isolated hospital wards, with genuinely infected patients. This would lead to a high risk of exposure to the virus in persons who were potentially vulnerable to the most severe effects of infection yet who otherwise were not (yet) infected themselves.

Despite the liberal use of high cycle thresholds, the requirement for unusually low numbers of DNA base-pairs, and no requirement for clinical diagnosis in the counting of cases during 2020 and early 2021, this changed once vaccines were rolled out. In the UK, the NHS instructed hospitals to only count people who were sick and symptomatic for COVID-19 as corona virus related admissions, previously they had counted anybody with a positive test [74]. The reason given was to improve accuracy in reporting the success of vaccines. Clearly the change in policy alone would result in a massive reduction of COVID-19 related hospital admissions being reported even if vaccines were entirely inconsequential; the press were silent about the matter. In July of 2021, a story emerged that suggested around 40% of people who were being counted as COVID-19 hospital admissions had actually been admitted to hospital for other causes, they were not sick with COVID-19 and merely tested positive as part of routine testing regimen [75]. It is unclear whether this method of counting was being applied to all patients or only the unvaccinated.

In May 2021, in the USA, the CDC also issued new guidelines for counting vaccine breakthrough cases (breakthrough cases are incidents where people who have been vaccinated later contract the disease they were vaccinated against) [60]:

As of May 1, 2021, CDC transitioned from monitoring all reported vaccine breakthrough cases to focus on identifying and investigating only hospitalized or fatal cases due to any cause. This shift will help maximize the quality of the data collected on cases of greatest clinical and public health importance.

A shift to only identifying, and monitoring, hospitalised or fatal cases would cause a huge difference to counting post-vaccine COVID-19 cases. The vast majority of 'cases' do not result in death and do not occur in people who need to be detained in hospital for treatment. If these changes were adopted, people with non-severe symptoms and those with none (asymptomatic), would not be counted. Why the sudden shift after over a year of doing things differently? Why did these changes in policy also coincide with the change in seasons and occur at a time when increasingly significant numbers of people had been vaccinated? Other changes in approaches to testing also occurred around this time.

In April 2021, the UK government rolled out a new national testing programme based on lateral flow tests after it had quietly dropped the widely publicised £100 billion 'operation moonshot' scheme. The aim was to increase the scope of testing by moving away from reliance on PCR with faster, easier to use, and more easily accessible tests. However, concerns about accuracy were raised early on with reports that as many as 98% of positive test results could be false in areas with low disease prevalence [76]. In the USA, reliability of the tests was deemed so poor by the FDA, that they refused authorisation for their use and publicly stated that the company who developed the test, Innova, had been misleading about claims for its efficacy [77].

Having signed a contract with Innova prior to testing the efficacy of their product, the UK Government ignored the issue and continued to use the tests despite evidence that they were less than 50% accurate in real-world use. However, it is worth noting that this damning analysis of the accuracy of the lateral flow tests was carried out via comparison with PCR tests using high cycle thresholds. An article in the Lancet attempted to clarify the issue. It suggested that the lateral flow tests were not designed to detect people who were not infectious - i.e., a positive test should not result from a low or no viable viral load, something which would occur with a PCR test run at a high cycle threshold, i.e., above 28 [78]. However, the author still noted that the lateral flow tests were not very reliable. Notably, the article also expressed frustration with regard to PCR protocols in use:

Remember, this is the PCR test that was used as the basis for declaring a pandemic and continued to be the core justification for locking down most of the planet.

Collective fear stimulates herd instinct and tends to produce ferocity toward those who are not regarded as members of the herd.

From 'Unpopular Essays' by Bertrand Russell

4. Deaths

a. Cycles of Fear

SARS-CoV-2 is said to have been isolated from respiratory tract samples taken in China at the beginning of 2020; the virus was reported to have been cultured on cells taken from human lung cancer patients [79]. The gene sequences taken from the samples formed the basis for the global testing program. A testing program that was integral to determining SARS-CoV-2 (the virus) as the causative factor in most of the deaths attributed to COVID-19 (the disease). Indeed, it is data from testing and associated deaths that supplied the WHO with the statistical information it used to declare a pandemic. Initially, the WHO had declared the emergence of the disease a 'Public Health Emergency of International Concern' (PHEIC). The pandemic was officially declared on the 11th of March 2021. Pandemic is scary word. Fear drives human behaviour in a very powerful way. For many, threats of death can instil the greatest fear. As shown in chapter 3, any testing regimen dependent on PCR tests carried out with a high cycle threshold is likely to prove very unreliable as a diagnostic. Yet the case count that led to a declaration of a pandemic, and the deaths attributed to the new disease, were fully dependent on PCR testing.

Government sponsored media fearmongering left the UK public terrorised. Many developed an extremely distorted perception of what was really happening. A poll, taken in the summer of 2020, suggested the public believed the death rate was 100 times higher than it actually was [80]. This was not just down to sensationalism but largely the result of deliberate government policy. The UK government had long made use of behavioural science and social psychology in order to control and manipulate public behaviour (a practice euphemistically known as 'nudging'). In 2010, the practice became more explicit with the formal organisation of a governmental group known as the Behavioural Insights Team; a group that later morphed into a private company partially owned by the Cabinet Office. Such a melding of private industry and the highest levels of government has significant parallels to the constructs involved in creating a top-down fascist state.

For the pandemic, a special behavioural science unit was established - the Scientific Pandemic Influenza Group on Behaviour (known as SPI-B). Their aim was to ensure that the public felt so threatened and terrorised that they would be compliant to government diktats in their behaviour. Members of the committee have since expressed their dismay at how the policy that emerged from the unit lacked ethics and was acting in a manner befitting an immoral totalitarian dictatorship [81]. Death, guilt, and vindictive social groupthink were at the core of their fear campaign. You will die or you will cause death by COVID-19 if you do not obey. You are heartless and uncaring if you do not obey. You will kill your frail elderly loved ones if you do not obey. And so on. A rapidly rising daily death count was one of their prime tools.

Malcolm Kendrick, who was working as a GP for the NHS in 2020, raised concern about the number of deaths that were being attributed to COVID-19 early on; many were being counted without any confirmatory test at all [82]. He expressed misgivings about the number of people being killed by lockdown policies rather than COVID-19 and he was also worried about the hysteria surrounding the virus; something which appeared to manifest as an implicit policy to inaccurately attribute as many deaths as possible to COVID-19. While many medical professionals were too busy, too terrorised, or too scared about their career to speak out, other lone voices such as Dr Renee Hoenderkamp, a London GP, made their concerns public too. In April 2020, an article she authored was published in Pulse - a magazine aimed at the General Practice community. In it she said [83]:

I am massively concerned that we are blinded by the headlights and the resultant deaths will be equalled if not excelled by other causes that we are now ignoring.

She was prompted to publicise her concerns after a number of her seriously ill patients had potentially life-saving treatment cancelled.

b. Deaths and Pandemic Policy

The ongoing death toll attributed to COVID-19, and deaths caused by lockdown policy, are topics that warrant further examination; especially those that occurred during the first wave in spring of 2020. What is particularly worrying is that a large number of first-wave deaths, those that appeared in the daily news in ever-increasing numbers, may not have been caused by SARS-CoV-2. In addition to concerns raised by medical professionals, a substantial number of relatives of people who died during the first wave felt strongly that their loved ones had been identified as COVID-19 deaths incorrectly and there were calls for an inquest [85]. An article published by the British Medical Journal supported their concerns. The author argued that out of 30 000 excess deaths that occurred during a five-week period in 2020, 20 000 were not attributable to COVID-19. They appeared to have been connected with lockdown policies such as the sudden removal of thousands of vulnerable patients from hospital care into community settings that were inappropriate to their needs [86]. Many of these patients were moved without first being tested. It is likely that many who were infected with COVID-19 were hurriedly placed in care settings where workers did not have access to suitable PPE and where they lacked adequate medical training. As a result of the move, large numbers of uninfected but vulnerable people would then have been exposed to, and infected by, SARS-CoV-2 [87]. Additionally, they were deprived of contact with loved ones and confined to their rooms where they had no access to fresh air and sunshine. These policies were challenged by key players in the industry who raised their concerns with government departments, including those under the direction of ministers Matt Hancock and Helen Whately. However, these concerns were ignored. In total, around 25 000 patients were moved from hospital into care homes before a mandatory testing scheme was put into place [88]. This move occurred in tandem with a blanket policy to impose 'do not resuscitate' orders on the elderly and people with learning disabilities without their consent or that of their relatives [89, 90]. Again, such a policy could only result in more deaths.

The Nuffield Trust calculated that around 40% of the 48 213 deaths that were attributed to COVID-19 during the first wave occurred in care homes [91]. It was also revealed that potentially life-saving treatment was withheld from disabled and chronically ill patients who were admitted into hospital; a fact made more disturbing by ONS figures which show that 60% of those who died following a positive corona virus test in the UK during 2020 were disabled [92]. Alarm has been raised over similar policies being deployed elsewhere in the world. For example, New York saw 9000 COVID-19 patients sent from hospitals directly into care homes [93]. Indeed, Matt Hancock defended his decision to send hospital patients into care homes on the basis that many other countries were doing the same [94]. It is not just policies concerning vulnerable patients and care homes that may have caused such a high death toll. Restrictions over the deployment of effective medicines and use of poor treatment techniques may also have contributed.

c. Ventilation

One treatment used on critically ill patients was ventilation; their inappropriate use appears to have contributed to an avoidable increase in deaths early in the pandemic. Medical professionals have suggested that the type of lung damage caused by COVID-19 made ventilation ineffective, inappropriate, and damaging - figures from New York suggest that up to four times more people may have died because of initial treatment policy that recommended mechanical ventilation too readily [95]. A treatment guide issued by the WHO in early March 2020, is one of the reasons mechanical ventilation was deployed. Mechanical ventilation was put forward as standard practice for use on patients with more severe respiratory difficulties [96]. However, there was a notable increase in survival rates once concerned doctors began to reject the use of ventilators in their treatment of COVID-19 patients [97, 98].

d. Midazolam

Another form of treatment that may have exacerbated death rates was use of a prescription sedative called Midalozam, a form of benzodiazepine. It is common practice to use it for palliative care, but expert opinion is that it should not be used in patients suffering from severe respiratory problems unless there is no chance of recovery [99]. This is because the drug relaxes muscles and makes breathing more difficult for those already struggling to respire. Use of Midazolam has also been associated with an increased risk of developing serious pneumonia [100]. In the UK during April 2020, double the number of prescriptions were issued for the drug when compared with previous years. Much of the extra volume of the drug appears to have been given to people in care homes who were suffering from more severe cases of COVID-19, or other respiratory diseases, and were already struggling for breath [101]. For any of these patients who may have had chance of recovering, the use of Midalozam could well have acted as a form of euthanasia. In July 2021, the Telegraph revealed that the placing people over the age of 70 into care homes and putting them on death pathways was part of a secret pandemic preparedness plan drawn up for the NHS in 2016; it was designed to prevent the NHS becoming overwhelmed [102]. Yes, the withdrawal of clinical care and the use of death pathways leading to a great number of fatalities was a policy designed to 'protect the NHS'.

e. Fatality rates

In March 2020, the director general of the WHO - Tedros Adhanom Ghebreyesus - declared that the global COVID-19 death rate was 3.4%, specifically noting that this was very serious because death rates from the flu were generally less than 1% [103]. At this point, the terms death rate, case fatality rate (CFR) and infection fatality rate (IFR) were being used with equivalence and interchangeably. It was this announcement by the WHO, alongside modelling based on this figure, that panicked many governments to consider, and then implement, draconian lockdown measures. Such measures included moving sick patients into care homes where they were without access to the professional medical care available in a hospital setting, isolated from human contact with friends and family, and deprived of fresh air and sunshine. However, the initial death rate figure used by the WHO was wrong by a considerable margin. Later analysis by Professor John P. A. Ioannidis, eventually published by the WHO in October of 2020 (five months after submission), confirmed that the infection fatality rate was more likely to be 1% or lower - similar to the flu [104]. A separate paper published by Professor Ioannidis concluded that the risk of death from COVID-19 in low-risk groups was roughly similar to that of the daily commute [105]:

People <65 years old have very small risks of COVID-19 death even in pandemic epicentres and deaths for people <65 years without underlying predisposing conditions are remarkably uncommon.

To understand the lethality of a disease it is important to be clear about some of the technical terms used (and misused) by health experts and scientists. Infection fatality rates and case fatality rates are different. Choosing one over the other can make a substantial difference to predictions and perceptions about the severity of an outbreak of infectious disease. An infection fatality rate (IFR) is used to refer to the number of people who die compared with the number estimated to have any type of infection, including those who may have gone undiagnosed having experienced only mild or unremarkable symptoms. A case fatality rate is used to refer to the number of people who die compared with those who have confirmed infections - generally those who display moderate to severe symptoms. This could become particularly confusing due to the way cases were being recorded for COVID-19, often based on unreliable tests performed on people with no symptomatic disease and a lack of clinical diagnosis. However, there is an essential point to be made. An IFR will generally have a much larger estimate of infections in a population compared to deaths and, as such, will tend to be a significantly lower ratio than a CFR. In the case of COVID-19, testimony before US congress that was intended to help inform early decision making on how to respond to COVID-19 compared the IFR of flu and the CFR of COVID-19, making out that the latter was ten times more deadly when it was not [106]. By March of 2021, the US CDC's analysis of IFR suggested it was best to consider age-banded figures. For the under 17s, the IFR was 0.002%, in the group of 18–49-year-olds it was 0.05%, between 50 and 64 years 0.6% and over 65 a much higher figure at 9% [107]. However, for many people even these figures are inaccurate estimates. As with any respiratory virus, those with other health issues are generally at far higher risk than those who are generally healthy. Professor John Ioannidis, an expert epidemiologist from Stanford University, analysed data from over 90 countries to reach a global average IFR of 0.15% [108].

Generally, high income countries with higher proportions of the population who are elderly have an IFR that is four or five times higher than low-income countries which have greater proportions of young people [109]. It is important to note that the IFR of evolving respiratory viruses can also change significantly during different years. Regardless, the initial response by the WHO and gross over-estimates of death rates may have contributed to public hysteria which is likely to have had significant psycho-social influence over medical professionals when determining cause of death.

One way of analysing whether COVID-19 deaths were being over-estimated would have been to use comparative analysis with deaths that were verified via post-mortem examination. However, such evidence is largely unavailable for most countries because very few post-mortems were carried out. Nonetheless, there is some evidence of deaths being over-counted. For example, Lawmakers in Minnesota believe that up to 40% of deaths had been misattributed to COVID-19 [110]. In June 2021, the Telegraph reported that a similar proportion of deaths were being misattributed to COVID-19 by the ONS, contravening WHO guidance [111]. If suspicions about vastly overestimated death counts are correct this would make the real IFR for COVID-19 substantially lower than published figures suggest.

f. Comparing Historical Mortality

Comparing the total number of deaths to previous years can be very misleading as populations can change in size, demography, and general levels of fitness. Excess death is a problematic concept because it is defined upon the basis of expectations - often based on comparatively short periods of time. The Office for National Statistics counts excess deaths as those running above the previous 5-year average. While the figure gives an idea of how the current year compares with recent mortality trends, the use of the word excess suggests that these deaths should have been avoidable. However, life is more complicated than that. Trends in any direction are rarely anomaly free and human experience shows that there are frequently incidents that lead to jumps in death rates. The ONS could choose any number of years from which an average number of deaths could be used as a comparison with the current year. Doing so would produce a different frame within which current mortality could be understood.

Excess death is effectively an arbitrary concept, but the use of excess death statistics can result in alarmist headlines. Comparisons to the early 20th century Spanish influenza pandemic or suggestions that mortality was worse than at any time since World War II were extremely unbalanced [112]. Such stories were designed to conjure fear. A more balanced analysis might have sought to understand death rates in the context of several factors. For example, comparison could be made with other years in which there were spikes in deaths. Patterns of economic decline could be considered. The influence of changes to NHS staffing and resourcing and a changing demography - such as increases in the number of elderly people – could be accounted for.

There is little doubt that 2020 saw a substantial spike in deaths but this fact is less dramatic if we consider context, including historical mortality rates, in a more sober light. As a matter of fact, deaths per 100 000 population in England and Wales were lower in 2020 than in 2003 and every preceding year [113]. Both 2015 and 2018 saw large numbers die due to seasonal disease including influenza in England and Wales. In fact, 2018 saw a whopping 154 000 deaths occur within the three-month period of January to March and 'excess' winter deaths were higher in 2018 than any year since 1975; yet life went on as usual [114]. Similarly, if we look at the deaths that occurred in 2008, we can see that 509 000 people died – 99 000 fewer than 2020 when 608 000 died [115]. However, the total population of England and Wales in 2008 was also around 5 million people fewer. England and Wales have seen the population increase by the equivalent of the entire population of Norway within 12 years. This means there are more people who might die. Additionally, the average age of the population had also risen.

So, in 2020 there were millions more people and proportionality many more elderly within the overall population. This means that when we look at age-standardised mortality we find a less sensational picture emerges. Age-standardised mortality makes adjustments for the proportion of elderly in a population and works from the number of deaths per 100 000 population. In England and Wales, 2008 saw an age-standardised mortality rate of 1091 per 100 000 - significantly higher than 2020 when it was 1043 per 100 000 [115]. In fact, 2008 and every year prior had higher age-standardised mortality rates than 2020 [113]; still undesirable but not quite so sensational or fear-inducing as some media headlines would have people believe.

Another facet of the pandemic propaganda involved the continuous highlighting of pressures on the NHS. However, the NHS was on its knees long before COVID-19. The total number of available hospital beds in England in 2020 was less than half that of the late 1980s [116, 117]. Between 2011 and 2020 around 15% of hospital beds were lost due to cuts and changing practice - around 20 000 in total. However, approximately 8000 of these beds were lost directly due to changes in bed arrangements attributed to pandemic infection control measures implemented in 2020. Yet these 'safety' measures were only made possible by removing elderly and disabled inpatients from hospital and placing them into care homes where they were deprived of expert medical care and where many became infected with SARS-CoV-2 and subsequently died. The rushed establishment of nightingale hospitals, costing over half a billion pounds, aimed to plug this reduction in capacity by making several thousand beds available. In practice only a few hundred beds were used; several of these hospitals did not treat a single COVID-19 patient. This was largely due to an omission in planning for a core functional component that was already in short supply in the NHS - the staff [118]. It is difficult to believe that the politicians and planners involved in creating these emergency units were not aware NHS resources, especially staff, were already stretched to their limit.

The preceding decades-long attack on NHS health care provision had long been symptomatic. In 2015, at least 30 000 patients were left waiting in ambulances for 30 minutes or more due to lack of capacity at accident and emergency; thousands of seriously ill patients were left for hours in hospital corridors without even being checked in or triaged, and there were reports of people dying as they waited long periods for an ambulance to arrive [119, 120, 121]. The same year, an ambulance crew dumped a dead body on the floor of an ambulance station because they had nowhere else to put it; the ambulance crew described their actions as normal practice [122]. Again, in 2016, huge queues of ambulances were found waiting outside hospitals to offload patients; something described by a paramedic as a frequent occurrence [123]. The paramedic in question was considering quitting due to exhaustion. Still things got worse.

Over the winter of 2016 - 2017, there was a 6000% increase in the number of patients waiting on trolleys in hospital corridors for 12 hours or longer [124]. Throughout 2017, seriously ill people were denied ambulances or continued waiting hours for them to turn up, some died waiting [125, 126, 127]. No remedial action was taken by the government and things appeared to continue to decline. In 2017 - 2018, the NHS was described as being in the worst winter crisis on record with severe bed shortages and reports of patients dying in corridors [128, 129]. Analysts observed how government-defined targets led to the production of statistics that distorted what was happening and could be used to cover over how bad things really were [130]. 2019 saw more reports: people waiting long periods for ambulances to arrive, sometimes leading to deaths; long queues of ambulances outside hospitals waiting to offload emergency patients; shortages of doctors and nurses; thousands of deaths due to lack of A&E capacity; and a large number of GP surgeries closing down permanently [131, 132, 133]. These declines in health service provision correlated with a notable deceleration in historical improvements to mortality rates in

England and Wales over the period 2011-2018 [114]. This mostly affected the most deprived sections of the population. The health service in England and Wales had little capacity to deal with any serious and unexpected large-scale health event immediately prior to 2020.

We have seen how the hastily implemented policy of removing vast numbers of elderly and disabled people from expert care and placing them into care homes with do not resuscitate orders may have contributed to a significant number of deaths. We have also seen how the NHS had long been cut to the bone by politicians obsessed with 'efficiency' leaving little capacity for national emergencies and we have seen how a more balanced context can help us understand that, while tragically high, death rates in 2020 were not as alarming as many made them out to be. In addition to this, we must also consider how COVID-19 deaths were being counted.

In England and Wales, anybody who died from any cause following a positive test were being counted as COVID-19 deaths. This was appalling due to reasons outlined already about the use of PCR testing and its lack of scientific credibility for use as a diagnostic. However, it also meant that anybody who ever tested positive would potentially be counted as a COVID-19 death. They could still have been counted under this method long after they had tested positive regardless of whether they had fully recovered or were asymptomatic. The BBC reported that somebody who died in a car crash months after a positive test would have been counted as a COVID-19 death [134]. Following a review, a new counting method was used which determined that anybody who died within 28 days of a positive test would be counted as a COVID-19 death [135]. This remained a poor and statistically unreliable means of measuring deaths. It still meant that people who died from almost any cause would be counted as a COVID-19 death on the sole basis of an unreliable and non-diagnostic PCR test.

In September 2020, a brief paper appeared in the Royal College of Physicians journal, 'Clinical Medicine' [136]. It attempted to address an ongoing debate concerning the difference between people who died *with* COVID-19 and those who died *of* COVID-19. The authors concluded that the vast majority of deceased hospitalised patients, whose deaths were attributed to COVID-19, died because of the virus. However, the main two pieces of evidence upon which they based this are highly questionable. The suggestion made by the authors was that x-rays showing pulmonary infiltration, plus the need for oxygen therapy, were conclusive proof that SARS-CoV-2 was the causative factor.

Pulmonary infiltration is simply evidence of a fluid or dense substance in the lungs, it is a medically imprecise term and diagnostically ambivalent. Pulmonary infiltration can be caused by a plethora of disease: influenza, pneumonia, bleeding on the lung from trauma (including intubation for ventilation), multiple sclerosis, kidney disease, hypertension, COPD and persistent bacterial infections to name but a few. Neither is the need for oxygen therapy a diagnostic measure, it is a treatment provided on the basis of a diagnostic measure - presumably low oxygen levels in the blood. Such symptoms could be caused by many things, especially in the elderly or those with underlying health conditions. There are serious questions to be asked if these were the key measures being used by clinical staff to determine cause of death. Some may object and suggest that, while medical professionals may not be 100% accurate, they would surely be correct most of the time. This is not the case. A pre-pandemic meta-analysis of research that examined the accuracy of clinical opinion on the cause of mortality found that at least one third of death certificates were inaccurate [137]. The study had compared clinically assigned causes of death with those determined by autopsies performed using microscopic examination. 50% of autopsies made findings that were completely unsuspected before death, although not all these findings contributed to a change in the primary cause of death. If serious inaccuracy was already an issue outside of the context of global hysteria and single-minded focus on one disease, it would surely have been a problem during it too.

g. Summary

The death rate for COVID-19 was used as a persistent tool to deliberately cause alarm, distress, and obedience among the UK population. Many of the deaths counted as COVID-19 deaths may have been misattributed. Many are likely to have been caused as a direct consequence of government policy and poor medical practice. Overall, excess mortality for

2020, when adjusted for age and a huge increase in total population, is far less alarming than many headlines had people believe. There is still excess mortality, of that there is no doubt, and aside from the reasons mentioned, lockdown policies and denial of care, examination, and services for non-COVID-19 related disease will have contributed enormously.

In January of 2020, the UK government designated COVID-19 as a High Consequence Infectious Disease (HCID), the criterion for which are [138]:

- Acute infectious disease.
- Typically has a high case-fatality rate.
- May not have effective prophylaxis or treatment.
- Often difficult to recognise and detect rapidly.
- Ability to spread in the community and within healthcare settings.
- Requires an enhanced individual, population, and system response to ensure it is managed effectively, efficiently, and safely.

Other diseases classed as an HCID in May 2020 included Ebola, Avian Flu, Lassa Fever, Monkeypox and the original SARS (caused by the virus SARS-CoV-1). However, the HCID status of COVID-19 was removed on the 19th of March 2020, 4 days before the implementation of the first UK lockdown. The reason given was [138]:

Now that more is known about COVID-19, the public health bodies in the UK have reviewed the most up to date information about COVID-19 against the UK HCID criteria. They have determined that several features have now changed; in particular, more information is available about mortality rates (low overall)...

5. Vaccines

a. Censorship, Corruption, and Bias

Vaccines were heralded as the road out of the pandemic very early on. Indeed, the focus and fervour on vaccines was so exclusive, it was clear that they were being positioned as the only true saviour that could return the populace to the promised land of life before the pandemic. Prophylactics and potential treatments were either ignored, downplayed, or disingenuously ridiculed. The suggestion that vaccines may herald their own set of problems and might not be the 'final solution' (as Bill Gates had called them during an interview on the Late Show [139]) were ridiculed and silenced regardless of the veracity of their scientific basis. (Bill Gates' comment was later edited out of the Late Show interview in an attempt to maintain his highly curated public persona.) Any modicum of scepticism, no matter how well founded, was usually labelled 'anti-vax' despite many highly qualified critics of the new technologies being deployed in corona virus vaccines being generally supportive of traditional vaccines. Their words of caution were responded to by vaccine fanatics with emotive venom, not calm logic and reasoning nor the tolerant acceptance of diverse opinion. This stance softened slightly with the later emergence of the phrase 'vaccine-hesitant', although the term was still deployed within contexts that made it implicit that those who had concerns over taking the vaccine were somehow misguided or mistaken. Unlike 'anti-vaxxers', who were portrayed as crazy and irrational, being 'vaccine hesitant' was framed as slightly more socially acceptable but ultimately, just like the 'anti-vaxxers', the 'vaccine-hesitant' were a group that needed to be re-educated and conquered, not listened to or, God-forbid, taken seriously. In the UK, there were significant additional efforts to connect a fall in deaths and cases with vaccination programs despite a dramatic seasonal drop in cases being expected and mirroring that of 2020 when zero vaccines were available.

Articles produced by mass media rarely cited the scientific background for the reasons people might hold for not wishing to take a vaccine. When such reasons were included, they were simplified into banal caricatures of the original concerns or deliberately confounded with more paranoid ideas about microchipping and gene editing [140, 141]. The media was being used as nothing more than a tool for obedience training. The stranglehold over what news reporters were permitted to report eventually led a group of 26 journalists to form a pressure group called 'Journalists Against Covid Censorship' claiming that information had been withheld or suppressed from the public including: discussions about the unreliability of PCR testing, effective treatments for COVID-19, the dreadful human toll attributable to draconian lockdown policies, and the many serious adverse side effects suffered by vaccine recipients [142].

In fact, many concerns about the vaccine were based on a combination of evidence. For example: the testimony of well qualified medical experts, peer-reviewed scientific publications, and decades of well-evidenced fraud and corruption within the pharmaceutical industry, health services, NGOs, governments, and national regulatory bodies. In general, the public are naive about how corrupt and biased science can be, especially when it comes to the influence of finance. Additionally, much science is not done, or analysed, in a balanced or realistic manner. For those interested, there are a number of books that can help shed some light on these issues including: 'Bad Science' by Ben Goldacre, 'Deadly Medicines and Organised Crime' by Peter Gotzsche, 'Science for Heretics' by Barrie Condon, or 'How to Lie with Statistics' by Darrell Huff. There is an overwhelming body of evidence that science is thoroughly corrupted, largely due to being performed in a culture which provides incentives and rewards for certain desired outcomes rather than 'true' ones [143]. The situation is so bad that many peer-reviewed research papers have been found to be based on data that has been manipulated or misrepresented so that false claims can be made that suit the agenda of the authors or their sponsors; many have been exposed for using data that has been completely fabricated - some estimates suggest fake data could be used in as much as 20% of published science [144]. In addition to human fallibilities, including egotism and greed, scientists are under immense institutionalised pressure to be popular, to attract funding, and to produce economically innovative technologies and products. A scientist who produces research suggesting that a technology in ubiquitous use, and that was once accepted as safe, is actually dangerous, is likely to find themselves being attacked, marginalised, and starved of funding.

The story of the immense power of the tobacco industry and how it harnessed science to distort, deceive, and distract for decades should be a warning to anybody who may be prone to mistakenly placing their trust in industry-backed science. None of this should be so surprising to a self-reflective and honest reader. On a personal level, much of the working public would privately admit that they are more likely to tow the line than to oppose or speak out against the unethical practices of their superiors for fear of losing their job. To some extent, we all speak the language of corporate BS even though for most of us it is superficial, vacuous, and nauseating. This is no different for scientists, or politicians for that matter. Most also have mortgages, families, ambitions, and reputations to consider. They are also subject to other forms of bias, pressure, and institutionalised thinking which can affect their cognition, consciously and unconsciously.

We must also consider the fact that the prevalence of clinical psychopathy within a given population could be anywhere from 1-4% [145]. This is not a joke. It means that as many as 1 in 25 people in general are likely to be psychopaths with high proportions in positions of power and influence [146]. Globally this would equate to the entire population of Britain, Australia, Canada, New Zealand, California, Texas, Florida, New York, Michigan, Washington, Ohio and Georgia combined. For these individuals, ethics and morals are things they neither understand nor have the capacity to care about. They understand social

44

rules as a game, and they use them to manipulate people via fake personas and public relations (propaganda). Psychopaths can feign the appearance of a well-adjusted ordinary person. For example, they will say they love their children without flinching while in reality, behind closed doors, they bully and abuse them. They are master manipulators and are likely to be highly functional in business and politics.

Some commentators suggest psychopaths may be useful in professions such as surgery where a cold clinical approach may be of benefit [147]. However, psychopath apologists simply do not understand psychopaths. They are always potentially dangerous to others. Those who do understand the dangers of psychopathy have called for screening to be carried out to prevent them being placed in positions where they can do significant harm to others, especially when this is potentially on a large scale [148]. Therefore, whether it is due to the danger of the influence of greed, the pressures of social and professional expectations, or full-blown psychopathy, we cannot assume that any person or organisation is beyond scrutiny. Conflicts of interest occur and must be brought to light and investigated. Research, statistics, decisions, policies, and law making must all be transparent and subject to challenge. Unfortunately, the fusion of government, regulators, and private industry, including the revolving door practices for making senior appointments, has normalised conflicts of interest and led to systems of governance that are unavoidably compromised. History warns us that science must be cross-examined in all aspects, especially when it is the bedfellow of political and economic interests, yet we have entered a period of authoritarian censorship, exclusion, and obfuscation, that is operating on a global scale.

Scandals involving asbestos, tobacco, and thalidomide are among the most controversial revelations of the 20th century. In all cases there was plenty of 'science' defending these products and it was many years, often decades, before the truth was exposed. The idea that there was no evidence for harm was commonly conflated with an assumption of safety. The impact that financial interests had on funding countless scientific studies that discounted any evidence for harm caused by tobacco is truly eye opening for anybody unfamiliar with the full saga. The key point is that science is for sale, it always has been, but the influence of industry-backed finance on government, regulatory bodies, and academic science is arguably greater now than it has ever been. We are also lacking a functioning free press with independent investigative journalists who are capable of in-depth scientific and political analysis unfettered by controlling editors.

All main sources of information are at the behest of corporate finance and billionaire owners. Government control over media content is also ubiquitous. It has sweeping legal powers that can prevent media from publishing information including the ability to enforce obedience through use of militarised security operations and closed courts. Governmental organisations such as the Scientific Pandemic Influenza Group on Behaviour, and military units such as 77th Brigade who specialise in psychological warfare, have worked at implementing obedience to government messaging through social and psychological techniques including the use of fake social media accounts to promote official narratives and harass and shame those with conflicting views [149]. Yes, it is a fact that a UK military unit has engaged in psychological warfare against the citizens of its own country. The government also uses taxpayer money to buy media influence. Since 2018, contracts worth £1.6 billion have been handed to one US media company alone (Omnicrom Inc.) [150]. Department of Health executive agency - Public Health England - became the largest single source of income to UK advertisers during 2020 [151].

It is therefore unsurprising that it is significantly challenging to find any popular news media article about COVID-19 vaccines that gives serious consideration to their potential harms. Subjects such as antibody dependent enhancement, vaccine-induced viral evolution, or vaccine-induced long-term chronic illness have been ignored. Nor has there been much pause for thought about the many scandals, conflicts of interest, and examples of corruption associated with pharmaceutical corporations within the context of COVID-19 vaccine testing and production. For example, the fact that Pfizer has been fined a record breaking $2.3 billion for a prolonged and deliberate fraud concerning the efficacy and safety of their products should be cause for concern about whether they can be trusted [152]. There was also scant mention of the sheer volume of pharmaceutical products recalled due to potential harmful effects. Between 2012 and 2019, 11,305 drug products were recalled in the US alone due to safety concerns [457]. 2,163 of these recalls occurred in 2019. These are products that passed preliminary trials, were assessed for risks and benefits, and had then been made available for treatment. Please think about the implications of what you have just read. Also ignored in mainstream coverage was any explanation of how many of those with concerns about Covid vaccines, including Nobel laureates, doctors, and other health professionals, were worried specifically about SARS-CoV-2 vaccines not about vaccination in general; a position feeble-minded journalists seemed unable to reconcile [153, 154, 155].

It is important to return to the fact that several companies developing and producing vaccines have been convicted multiple times for fraud and deception. History has shown repeatedly that the most monstrous and demonic events take place following deliberate deception by a few, accompanied by the blind trust and herd mentality of the many. Dogmatic ideology is often lurking in the shadows, but personal financial profit, career progression, perceived esteem, protecting one's current standing, or simply fear of standing out are all that is required to motivate people to align with perceived expected behaviours. Therefore, being diligent in your dealings with powerful people or organisations is not only common-sense advice, it is a civic duty. This is especially so if you are making a decision, or encouraging others to decide, about penetrating the body to inject something into the flesh and blood that may have irreversible biological effects, one of which could be death. However, if you knew the supplier of such a product was a criminal with multiple convictions, and those pushing the product had a track record for unethical, dishonest behaviour, would it be unreasonable to simply decide not to have any dealings with that party at all? Would it be unreasonable to mistrust the product they were pushing even if the first couple of samples were freebies? (Actually not free but paid for by taxpayers).

First, let's see if the vaccine manufacturers stand up to scrutiny. Since 2000, in the US alone, AstraZeneca have been subject to 21 successful prosecutions for unlawful behaviour incurring over $1.3 billion in fines [156]. During the same period, Johnson and Johnson have exhibited far worse behaviour. They have accumulated 58 penalties resulting in over $4 billion in fines [157]. However, Pfizer top the league of the three with over 71 transgressions, resulting in total fines in excess of $4.6 billion [158]. Violations committed by all three of these companies include anti-competitive practices, bribery (or making improper payments), and misrepresenting the safety, efficacy, and applicability of their products. Providing kickbacks and other benefits to doctors and government officials in return for contracts, making prescriptions, and promoting their products, is commonplace.

In the UK, Pfizer have also been caught price gouging. They were involved in altering the branding of an important anti-epileptic drug and then increasing the price by almost 2600%. A move intended to enrich Pfizer's revenue stream at a cost to the NHS of an additional £48 million [159]. As of 2020, Moderna's track record was blemish free – the company was only incorporated in 2010 and they had never previously produced a commercially viable product. Many of their experiments with gene-based medicine failed to reach phase III trials due to serious safety concerns raised during animal experiments. High staff turnover and scientific secrecy led to speculation that the priorities of CEO, salesman Stephane Bancel, run roughshod over biological science and medical professionalism [160]. However, his impatience to bring a product to market was relieved in 2020. Firstly, former Moderna board member Dr Moncef Slaoui was appointed to lead the USA's national COVID-19 vaccine programme - operation warp speed. Then followed the approval of the Moderna vaccine (for emergency use only). Forecast revenues from their COVID-19 vaccine are in the region of $18 billion and their share price increased tenfold in 2020 [162]. This led AstraZeneca to sell their 7.7% stake in Moderna for over $1 billion - more than four times their initial investment [161]. Moderna company executives were also able to cash in over $180 million worth of stock in 2020 [162]. Both events suggested that those with inside knowledge may not be expecting the share price to continue rising.

Novavax is a US corporation focused on producing vaccines. Prior to 2020 the company had not released a single commercial vaccine since being founded in 1987. In 2015, Novavax received $89 million from the Bill and Melinda Gates Foundation. However, the company had still been in difficult financial circumstances due to its failure to bring to market a safe and effective vaccine. This may be due to a more rigorous approach, overly ambitious attempts to tackle challenging emerging viruses such as Ebola, SARS and MERS, or novel attempts to use plant-based chemicals as adjuvants, and insect cells for viral protein culture [163]. However, reports suggest Novavax had rushed experiments and all of its previous vaccine candidates failed in trials [164]. At least this suggests their design, management and analysis of trial data has had some integrity rather than the frequent industry practice of hiding unwanted trial results and fudging data to help bring products to market. In 2020 the company's fortunes changed. The corona virus pandemic saw them receive around $2 billion in funding, most of which came via the US government. Its share price went from under $5 dollars at the end of 2019, to a peak of $290 in February 2021 after which it fell back a little [165]. The Novavax corona virus vaccine appears likely to be combined with its novel flu vaccine for roll out in time for winter 2021. It is notable that developing its flu vaccine to a market-ready phase took ten years. More than five times longer than has been spent on developing its COVID-19 vaccine.

Vaccines pushed in the UK were procured by a government acting on advice from the MHRA and SAGE. The government itself is staffed at its most senior levels by persons mired in illegal and unethical conduct. The health secretary in 2020, Matt Hancock, was a politics, philosophy, and economics graduate. He had no experience or qualifications relating to science or medicine. In 2021, following a court case pursued by an NGO, Hancock was found to have broken the law, and his own government's ethical standards, in his handling of generous taxpayer funded contracts [166]. One notable NHS contract was awarded to his friend and neighbour who had till that point only dealt in catering supplies [167]. Hancock was also caught breaking the social distancing restrictions he had helped impose when footage emerged of him embracing a married woman while at work [168]. Hancock, who had previously threatened holidaymakers with ten years in jail for completing a form incorrectly, was himself married at the time of the incident [169]. Perversely, Hancock had previously served on a parliamentary Standards and Privileges Committee and acted as a governmental anti-corruption champion. The father of Hancock's lover, Rino Coldangelo, holds, or has held, directorships in several pharmaceutical or biomedical companies including Harrison Life Sciences Group who, among other things, are involved in the supply of antibody reagents – a core component of disease testing kits. Hancock's sister and her husband run a 'security services' company based in Wrexham called

Topwood Ltd (company number 04398739); their activities include document scanning, storage, and shredding. In 2019, following Hancock's appointment as Secretary of State for Health and Social Care in 2018, Topwood Ltd were awarded an NHS contract via NHS Shared Business Services Ltd - a company set up by the government Department of Health and Social Care in 2005 as part of the creeping privatisation of the NHS.

Prime minister Boris Johnson (full name Alexander Boris De Pfeffel Johnson) appointed his fellow Oxford alumni, Matthew John David Hancock, to the position of Secretary of State for Health and Social Care. Like Hancock, Johnson also has a record of abusing the law. Johnson was a member of the Bullingdon club (as was former prime minister Cameron). At that time, the Bullingdon club consisted of a group of over-privileged spivs who entertained themselves in the manner of a gang of adolescent psychopaths - by dressing up as Nazis, hiring prostitutes, belittling women, abusing ordinary members of the public (who were branded 'plebs'), and having micro-riots, one of which was alleged to have involved smashing a restaurant window [170, 171]. Were it not for their privileged status, Johnson and his chums would most likely have criminal records and be under surveillance via use of the gang violence matrix used by police intelligence.

In 2014, during his period as Mayor of London, Johnson squandered hundreds of thousands of pounds buying and renovating three mobile water cannons that were later banned from use and sold for scrap [172]. Presumably he had anticipated that these would be used for controlling public disorder resulting from the implementation of Conservative party policies. In 2019, the Supreme court found Johnson guilty of unlawfully suspending parliament in spring of that year, acting in breach of one of the most fundamental elements of the UK's constitution [173]. It was a profound decision, exposing a government that was had no respect for the most basic fundamentals of the rule of law. It should have shaken the British people to their core and brought the government down. However, the incident barely registered with a public mesmerised by profane propaganda, unaware of their own constitution, and utterly desensitized to corruption. Late in 2019, he retained his position as PM via election by the plebiscite. In 2020, he went on to breach international law by reneguing on elements of the EU withdrawal agreement [174].

In 2021, it came to light that Johnson had spent £200 000 decorating his flat at Downing Street, exceeding the already generous annual allowance of £30 000 allocated from taxpayer's money [175]. There were calls for an inquiry into the origin of the funds. Johnson duly obliged. Not by submitting to an independent inquiry, but by personally appointing Lord Geidt as a ministerial standards advisor. Lord Geidt was a typical member of the establishment - a privately educated Cambridge graduate who had served in the Royal Household for well over a decade. Despite this, Johnson still limited Geidt's remit and prevented him from being able to launch his own inquiries independently [176]. Unsurprisingly, Geidt's inquiry found that Johnson's actions were unwise but not unlawful. Which is a diplomatic and chummy way of saying that Johnson was morally corrupt but there was nothing anybody could do about it. The attempted whitewash did not succeed entirely and mounting pressure forced Johnson to appoint additional members to the committee for standards in public life. One of his selections - Ewen Fergusson, a former Bullingdon club member and personal friend of Johnson from his university days - made it clear what the true purpose of the committee was going to be [177].

Other significant conflicts of interest abound in the advisory groups set up to advise the UK government on its pandemic response. For example, Kate Bingham, chair of the vaccine taskforce (VTF) was appointed while she was still a managing partner for an investment firm with key holdings in pharmaceutical companies [178], and both Patrick Vallance and John Bell were found to have significant numbers of shares in companies that were awarded high value vaccine and testing contracts [179]. Most of the key influential figures involved in SAGE (Scientific Advisory Group for Emergencies), the group that directed government policy for the pandemic, have worked for pharmaceutical companies or received significant amounts of money for research from the funding organisations of influential financiers such as the Bill and Melinda Gates Foundation and the Wellcome Trust. Between 2014 and 2018, the Bill and Melinda Gates Foundation (BMGF) provided a whopping $744 million to UK universities; primary recipients included Oxford University ($166 million) and Imperial College ($133 million) [180]. This funding was part of a BMGF 'decade of vaccines' that involved distributing $10 billion in funding commencing in 2010 and ending, coincidentally, just prior to the SARS-CoV-2 outbreak in 2020 [181]. At least a further $1.75 billion has been made available by the BMGF to help develop products in response to COVID-19; the CEO of the BMGF made it clear that this funding was short-term and aimed at being a catalyst to market development [182]. Another notable donation made by the BMGF was one of almost £1 million made to the MHRA in 2017 [183].

The MHRA (Medicines and Healthcare Products Regulatory Agency) is the UK agency for the oversight of drugs and medicines. Its funding comes entirely from private capital - mostly from the pharmaceutical industry. The relationship between the two has long been identified as problematic. In 2004, it was revealed that industry representatives were preparing diktats on how the agency should be run, including a desire to increase industry representation within the MHRA, and the MHRA had engaged in joint lobbying campaigns to support the commercial interests of the industry in Europe, indicating signs of regulatory capture [184]. Regulatory capture occurs when a government, or non-governmental regulator, becomes ineffective due to becoming too intertwined with the industry it is supposed to regulate. This can occur either through direct or indirect financial interests and/or the ideologies, personal relationships, and career ambitions of individuals employed or contracted by regulators.

A trusting individual may see no issue over who funds what, but this is a terribly naive viewpoint. Money always has intentions - usually those intentions are tied to the people providing the money. It is clear that the UK government and pandemic response groups are generally comprised of establishment figures. As such, there will inevitably be a hegemonic culture emerging from these groups and pertaining to the advice they give. Anybody truly independent would not form part of the establishment and so is unlikely to be involved. There is no need to imagine grand conspiracies between multiple actors here. Just a collusion of personal and professional interests that are consciously or otherwise guided by cash flow will suffice to see alternative viewpoints excluded or blocked. Over protracted periods of time, whole academic disciplines will inevitably be captured in their own reinforcing echo chambers. Many of those involved will undoubtedly hold a genuine belief in their own opinions and the guidance they are giving to others. Thomas Kuhn's work on scientific paradigms provides on explanation of the matrix that shapes and holds beliefs in certain patterns, including how paradigms become entrenched through dogmatic approaches to education. However, when you add the powerful influence of funding, something Kuhn's theories fail to grapple with, paradigms become increasingly dogmatic, impossible to criticise, and equally hard to shift. This will be even more difficult when those funding scientific work spread their influence into other arenas too. It may be uncommon knowledge, but the BMGF has funded far more than science and education. Donations totalling $250 million have also been made to multiple media companies including the BBC, Al Jazeera, the Guardian, and the Financial Times; other recipients include 'fact checkers' such as PolitiFact [185]. The danger here is that the billions and billions pumped into science, the media, fact checkers, and many other organisations, including think tanks, and policy forums, could easily shape and shepherd the thinking of both the scientific community and the general public.

b. A Violation of Internationally Agreed Ethics

During the COVID-19 pandemic, there has been the emergence of a type of group-think - a tyrannical technocratic narrative about whether it is best to persuade people to take the vaccine, or just to force them to take it instead [186]. Re-education camps may be reserved for the last remnants of the 'vaccine hesitant' who are able to resist the coercive threats of having draconian disadvantages imposed upon them, such as limitations on employment, travel, and socialising. In the US, the CDC pushed a rule to force the unvaccinated to wear masks - the vaccinated were exempt [187]. This is deeply manipulative social psychology that aims to force people to wear a dehumanising physical symbol associated with silencing, shame, and disease, in order to identify them as an out-group. The cultivation of this social division took place during 2020 and 2021 while the vaccine was, by any commonly accepted definition of the word, experimental. It was not possible for long-term safety or efficacy to have been assessed using empirical evidence - the treatment was too novel for any such studies to have been carried out; you can speed up trials, but you can't speed up time or travel into the future.

The National Institutes of Health (NIH) had listed the expected completion date for the clinical trials for the Pfizer COVID-19 vaccine as May 2022 [188]. As of July 2021, no trial data had been submitted to the NIH by Pfizer. Later in this section, many more reasons for considering the vaccines experimental will also be discussed. What is particularly alarming is that a majority of the public seem to have shown little concern over, or resistance to, the use of overt and covert propaganda, manipulation, imposed disadvantage, and coercion, to force people into having an experimental medical intervention. In fact, many seemed to enjoy the opportunity to view unvaccinated people as an unhygienic out-group to avoid; a group deserving of hatred that should be put on public shaming lists, monitored, psychologically bullied, physically harassed, and refused essential medical treatment [189, 190, 191].

Despite claims to the contrary, what has happened is in contravention of the Nuremberg code which states [192]:

...the person involved should have legal capacity to give consent; should be so situated as to be able to exercise free power of choice, without the intervention of any element of force, fraud, deceit, duress, over-reaching, or other ulterior form of constraint or coercion; and should have sufficient knowledge and comprehension of the elements of the subject matter involved as to enable him to make an understanding and enlightened decision. This latter element requires that before the acceptance of an affirmative decision by the experimental subject there should be made known to him the nature, duration, and purpose of the experiment; the method and means by which it is to be conducted; all inconveniences and hazards reasonable to be expected; and the effects upon his health or person which may possibly come from his participation in the experiment.

It also contravenes Article 7 of the UN Covenant on Civil and Political Rights:

Most explicitly, and not contingent on arguments about whether the vaccines were experimental, arguments based on the greater good, collective responsibility, or civic duty, are directly in contravention of UNESCO's Universal Declaration on Bioethics and Human Rights, Article 3, part 2 [193]:

The interests and welfare of the individual should have priority over the sole interest of science or society.

In January of 2021, the Council of Europe - an organisation designed to uphold human rights internationally, and which the UK helped found following World War 2 - passed resolution 2361. It included the following statements concerning COVID-19 vaccines [458]:

7.3.1 ensure that citizens are informed that the vaccination is not mandatory and that no one is under political, social or other pressure to be vaccinated if they do not wish to do so;

7.3.2 ensure that no one is discriminated against for not having been vaccinated, due to possible health risks or not wanting to be vaccinated.

It is patently clear that the prevailing pre-pandemic western consensus on medical ethics places prime value on individual choice and rights. A fact agreed upon by an internationally recognised organisation of which the UK was a founding member and who have made specific reference to the importance of not mandating COVID-19 vaccines. This should be considered valid international law that is binding on all member states. Historically, such values were deemed so important people fought and gave their lives to defend them. The reasons were once clear - to respect freedom and personal integrity, to avoid the imposition of medical fascism, and to prevent repeating the sort of massive injustice and harm we have witnessed in our not-too-distant history. Values and lessons that have now been carelessly abandoned. In the USA, the states of Florida and Texas held these rights to be so important that they banned vaccine passports, or the imposition of any system that might coerce people into taking a medication by forcing people to disclose their private medical information during the course of their daily lives [194].

When it comes to COVID-19 vaccines, the issue of informed consent is particularly troubling. Having a corrupt politician or unqualified, woolly-minded celebrity say, 'it's safe and effective' or 'just get the jab' with a dismissive sneer or a wave of the arm certainly does not qualify as informed consent. Nor does it justify forcibly holding a patient down and injecting them through their clothes against their will as has happened in Scotland [195]. Some people thought this was acceptable; we are truly in dangerous times.

The immune system is not the simple machine one might believe it to be after seeing one of the many simplified cartoons used to explain how vaccines work. These cartoons were designed in order to encourage uptake not to educate or inform. The truth is that medical science still has much to learn about the immune system including the full complexity of genome-environment interactions, epigenetic interplay, autoimmunity, disease resistance, and trans-generational effects. Furthermore, vaccines using mRNA technology have never previously been approved for use on humans even in an emergency context, nor had the vaccines being launched been subject to multiple, rigorous, replicated, double-blinded, longitudinal studies [196]. Initial trials also excluded vulnerable groups including pregnant women, the elderly, and those with serious illness. Some intermediary papers were published following the first and/or second stages of the trials but full data was not published with them. Ordinarily, a vaccine can take a decade or longer to develop, test, and bring to market [197].

In effect, the launch of the vaccine program was simply an extension of the experimental trials that were still ongoing. There was certainly no risk-benefit analysis, nor could there be a realistic one when you simply do not have adequate information about positive and negative long-term effects. Some may argue it was necessary to take a chance with the vaccines given the threat of corona virus, but this gamble is based on hope not science. It is effectively a blind leap of faith. It was also largely based on the social and economic pressures caused by lockdown rather than simply fear of the disease itself. The dominant narrative was that vaccines for all would be the only way out of a government imposed medical tyranny. This is simply untrue. However, with the world experiencing an onslaught of fear-inducing propaganda and varying degrees of curfew and totalitarian-style governance, it is easy to understand why vaccines have taken on a quasi-religious role. While SARS-CoV-2 does appear to cause a real and deadly disease, the threat it poses has been deliberately exaggerated and the efficacy of natural immunity, prophylactics, and treatments have been downplayed or ignored completely; as have the cumulative long-term consequences of lockdown or the vaccine program itself.

Serious concerns about vaccines were raised early on by numerous scientists and independent commentators. While some fringe elements made wild and contentious claims, many concerns were genuine and based on scientific knowledge, clinical experience, and peer-reviewed evidence, yet none of this science was given the serious space and discussion it deserved by the popular media; instead, it was censored. This draconian control of information and news was dominant across multiple popular resources including Facebook, Twitter, and YouTube [198, 199, 200, 201].

Facebook fired an employee who blew the whistle on censorship policies by leaking evidence of the development of algorithms to effect a shadow ban on posts with content that might lead anybody to question the need, safety, or efficacy of the vaccines [202]. Information was kept hidden from view or removed regardless of whether it was fact, a scientifically supported opinion, a link to a peer reviewed science journal, the opinion of qualified medical professionals or an accurate empirical report from personal experience. Search results were filtered, posts were removed or shadow-banned, and social media accounts and channels erased completely. Anything that did not support the narrative dictated by the authorities was fair game for repression.

c. Natural Immunity

For much of the pandemic, but especially following the rollout of vaccines, a false narrative was used to suggest that effective immunity can only be achieved through vaccination. This idea was blatantly false, as was the notion that herd immunity could only be achieved through vaccination. The World Health Organisation had explicitly acknowledged the role of non-vaccine acquired immunity in reaching the all-important goal of herd immunity [203]:

> *'Herd immunity', also known as 'population immunity', is the indirect protection from an infectious disease that happens when a population is immune **either** [emphasis added] through vaccination or immunity developed through previous infection.*

Previous infection does not need to have been with SARS-CoV-2. Cross-reactivity is the name given when exposure to one pathogen can produce a response against another one. A classic example is the immunity derived against smallpox from cowpox exposure - a discovery that led to directly to modern vaccines (the word vaccine is derived from the Latin 'vacca' - meaning cow). The likelihood of cross-reactive immunity from corona viruses, including those that cause the common cold and also the more serious SARS-CoV and MERS-CoV, was suspected, and highlighted, at least as early as June 2020 [204]. Those suspicions proved correct. In November 2020, a study was published in the 'Journal of Clinical Investigation' that examined cross-reactivity to SARS-CoV-2 that had arisen following exposure to other similar viruses [205]. The conclusion of the study was that 90% of people who had not previously been exposed to SARS-CoV-2 exhibited positive antibody responses. Measures were taken to ensure that this was not due to prior asymptomatic exposure to SARS-CoV-2. As such, the presence of cross-reactive immunity was believed likely due to prior exposure to other corona viruses in circulation - four of which are known to be associated with causing the common cold.

In addition to cross-reactive immunity, people exposed to SARS-CoV-2 are very likely to have developed virus-specific immunity. A fact that was even acknowledged by the UK's Office for National Statistics. On July 7th, 2021, they released a report suggesting that

90% of the UK public had developed antibodies to SARS-CoV-2 either from vaccination or prior infection [206]. They also stipulated that an absence of antibodies:

...does not mean that a person has no protection against COVID-19, as an immune response does not rely on the presence of antibodies alone.

This is a crucial point but does not receive adequate further attention either in the ONS report (which appears to be aimed solely at encouraging vaccination) or in popular media. It is notable that the core SAGE committee formed in the UK at the beginning of its pandemic response did not include a single immunologist - a field that is concerned with long-term immunity [207]. The fact is that many people already had robust immunity to SARS-CoV-2 without vaccination [208]. Plus, people with natural immunity are no more likely to pose an infection risk to others than fully vaccinated people, possibly less due to the enhanced risk of dangerous viral evolution occurring in vaccinated people (see chapter 5, section e, vii).

Immunity derived from a natural infection also appears to be much broader, more robust, and almost certainly longer lasting than vaccine-acquired immunity. In part, this is because it induces production of a wider set of immune components including the presence of IgA (immunoglobulin A) at mucosal sites - an important barrier to viral entry into deeper tissue; something that vaccines designed to produce spike protein antigens do not achieve [209, 210]. If a natural immune response occurs upon exposure to the virus, it is generally robust regardless of the severity of infection; there are a minority of people, generally the more aged, whose immune system does not respond, but they are equally unlikely to benefit from vaccination yet will still be at risk from side effects [210, 211]. Additionally, as reported in the publication 'Nature', there is evidence that natural immunity from prior infection may be long-term, possibly life-long, following confirmation of the presence of antigen-specific long-lived bone marrow plasma cells in people who recovered from SARS-CoV-2 infections [212, 213]. This research highlights the fact that it is not necessary to have detectable antibodies for immunity to be present. The idea that low antibody levels equal reduced long-term immunity is simply false. Following exposure to an antigen, the body will usually produce a high level of antibodies but once the invader is believed to have been controlled and defeated, there is no need to retain a high level of antibodies. It would be unnecessary, ineffective, and probably impossible for the body to retain high levels of antibodies for all the infectious elements it is exposed to over its lifetime. Instead, following an aeon of evolution, the immune system has developed clever mechanisms to store a memory of the invader which will enable it to quickly produce antibodies in the future should re-exposure occur. This allows it to drop the levels of actual circulating antibodies to a very low level which may not be detectable. In July 2021, analysis of a large dataset from Israel indicated that 40% of people with new COVID-19 infections were vaccinated compared with just 1% who had previously recovered from the disease [214].

In August 2021, the ONS reported that over 90% of adults in the UK would test positive for antibodies against SARS-CoV-2 [215]. Remember that people who do not test positive for antibodies following recovery from a natural infection can still be immune, either through non-specific immunity, by carrying antibodies that are not detected by the test, or having capacity to make antibodies following activation of immune memory cells. By contrast, an article in the Telegraph, also published in August 2021, reported that Professor Andrew Pollard - the lead on the Oxford vaccine team - had accepted that it was clear that vaccines did not prevent people from contracting a SARS-CoV-2 infection [216]. This meant that the vaccinated remained a potential source of spread, and that vaccine-acquired herd immunity was therefore unachievable. It also meant that the idea of vaccine passports was not supported by scientific reasoning. A policy that required only unvaccinated people to be forced to isolate if they came into contact with a person who had a positive test would therefore be irrational, discriminatory, and have potential to cause massive spread of the virus via vaccinated people, with potential for more pathogenic mutations arising as a result (refer to the later section on vaccine-induced viral evolution).

In summary, natural immunity is real, robust, and long lasting. It does not require prior exposure to same virus it protects from, so a prior positive test for SARS-CoV-2 is not a necessary indicator for natural immunity. Natural immunity confers protection on both the individual and the community. Negative antibody tests do not exclude the presence of natural immunity. If people have functioning natural immunity to a virus, the risk / benefit of taking a vaccine becomes all risk. No matter how low this risk might appear to be, it is an unnecessary risk. Neither does a functioning level of immunity need to be 'boosted'. Indeed, not only do vaccines carry some risk of adverse effects, the simple act of overstimulating the immune system can itself be damaging; in some cases, leading to chronic immunological disorders. Plus, there is an economic and environmental cost to producing, storing, transporting, and administering a vaccine.

d. What is in the Experimental Vaccines?

Vaccines designed to protect against COVID-19 were, de facto, experimental when they were rolled out to be used on the public in the largest mass vaccination campaign in history. The Human Medicines Regulations 2012 would have prevented their use save for regulation 174 which states that temporary emergency authorisation may be given to products designed to protect against pathogenic spread. The use of regulation 174 is evidence that the vaccines were neither fully approved, nor proven safe and effective in the medium and long-term. As of mid-July 2021, government issued advice for healthcare professionals concerning the AstraZeneca vaccine's regulation 174 status, stated clearly [217]:

The duration of protection afforded by the vaccine is unknown as it is still being determined by ongoing clinical trials.

It also stated:

This product contains GMOs.

As of June 2021, the government advice to healthcare professionals concerning the Pfizer vaccine's regulation 174 status was devoid of any mention of long-term efficacy whatsoever. One thing it did say was [218]:

In the absence of compatibility studies, this medicinal product must not be mixed with other medicinal products.

This meant that it should not be injected if a person has other active medicines in their body. There were no exceptions to this. At the time this advice was given, neither vaccine had been granted a marketing number - because they were not fully approved.

The disclosed ingredients for the vaccines that were in use in the UK as of July 2021 are listed below [219, 220, 221, 222]. Neither Moderna's proprietary SM-102, nor the PEG (polyethylene glycol) used in Pfizer's product, have ever previously been used in an approved vaccine. Nor had any of the main active ingredients, or any listed combination of excipients, ever been used in humans prior to the deployment of these inoculants.

<u>Pfizer/BioNTech (BNT162b2):</u>

- BNT162b2 single stranded mRNA
- ALC-0315 = ([(4-hydroxybutyl)azanediyl]di(hexane-6,1-diyl) bis(2-hexyldecanoate))
- ALC-0159 = 2-[(polyethylene glycol)-2000]-N,N-ditetradecylacetamide
- 1,2-Distearoyl-sn-glycero-3-phosphocholine (DSPC)
- Cholesterol
- Potassium chloride
- Potassium dihydrogen phosphate
- Sodium chloride
- Disodium hydrogen phosphate dihydrate
- Sucrose
- Water

<u>AstraZeneca sold as Vaxzevria / Covishield:</u>

- ChAdOx1-S recombinant particles (modified chimpanzee adenovirus) produced in genetically modified human embryonic kidney (HEK) cells (HEK 293).
- L-Histidine
- L-Histidine hydrochloride monohydrate
- Magnesium chloride hexahydrate
- Polysorbate 80 (E433)

- Ethanol

- Sucrose

- Sodium chloride

- Disodium edetate dihydrate

- Water

Moderna:

- Single stranded mRNA

- Lipid SM-102

- Cholesterol

- 1,2-distearoyl-sn-glycero-3-phosphocholine (DSPC)

- 1,2-dimyristoyl-rac-glycero-3-methoxylpolyethylene glycol-2000 (PEG2000-DMG)

- Trometamol

- Trometamol hydrochloride

- Acetic acid

- Sucrose

- Water

Janssen (Johnson & Johnson):

- Adenovirus type 26 encoding the SARS-CoV-2 spike glycoprotein

- 2-hydroxypropyl-B-cyclodextrin

- Citric acid monohydrate

- Ethanol

- Hydrochloric acid

- Polysorbate 80

- Sodium chloride

- Sodium hydroxide

- Trisodium citrate dihydrate

- Water

e. COVID-19 Vaccine Risks

i. Risk, Benefit and Significant Under-Reporting of Adverse Events

A deliberate disinformation narrative was used by public health spokespersons to promote vaccine uptake. This narrative suggested that adverse event data was being properly analysed, showed no concerning trends when compared with ordinary background incidence of reported events, and that reporting would be overzealous due to the novel nature of the vaccine. Zero evidence was offered in support of this. In fact, as we shall see, a body of research shows that this narrative was unscientific and based on poor assumptions. Many adverse reactions were unreported, but it is not clear how many. It should be very few because government guidance was clear from the outset; the novel vaccines were classed as a 'black triangle' medicine - meaning they required health professionals to be especially vigilant in spotting and reporting harmful effects. Additionally, the 'Green Book' - an authoritative source of government guidance - is clear that uncertainty over whether an adverse reaction was or was not connected with a vaccination does not constitute a reason to avoid submitting a report no matter how minor the reaction [223]:

The MHRA encourages reporting of suspected ADRs even if there is uncertainty as to whether the vaccine played a causal role.

And:

...all serious and non-serious suspected ADRs should be reported, for both adults and children.

However, research has shown that the vast majority of adverse drug reactions, including the most serious ones, are not reported. Of those that are, the information supplied is frequently of poor quality. For example, one study found that UK medical practitioners frequently did not report adverse drug reactions. The reasons given included, not having sufficient time, and holding the false belief that reports should only be submitted where there was no doubt that the only possible cause was the medication [224]. This research also showed that doctors appeared to have little understanding about what the Yellow Card reporting scheme was for nor what the black triangle signified. This study is quite dated but contemporary evidence does not conflict with its findings. A more recent systematic review of 47 published research papers identified the under-reporting of adverse effects as a major problem that was closely linked with attitudinal responses of the medical professionals concerned [225]. Lack of time was a major factor used to excuse themselves of any duty to submit reports, but other more disturbing excuses given included: indifference - described as the belief that one more (or less) report wouldn't make a difference; and complacency based on the belief that only safe drugs were allowed on the market! These last two excuses are perhaps the most startling and reveal that some medics lack any modicum of professionalism, are devoid of even a basic understanding of statistical principles, and imbue a level of naivety belittling of the intelligence supposedly required to qualify for practice. Either that or they hold irrational biases they dare not see challenged and so they behave in improper ways that will bolster their assumptions rather than challenge them.

A study conducted in Canada provided evidence that patients were more likely to report side effects to medical professionals rather than attempt to do so directly, yet when they do, medical professionals downplay side effects and dismiss concerns rather than take them seriously and submit an official report [226]. Globally, research has shown that health professionals are significantly more likely to report positive attitudes toward the need for reporting detrimental effects that may be linked to medication than to actually do it in practice [227].

The Yellow Card scheme was implemented following the Thalidomide scandal of the 1960s [228]. This drug, used to treat morning sickness, was given to pregnant women on the basis of industry-funded research proving that it was safe and effective. It was used for years before the safety issues came to light and action was taken to ban the drug. The consequence was that thousands of babies were born with defects that would confer upon them a serious lifelong disability. The yellow card scheme was intended for use without placing any burden of correlating clinical evidence on the person reporting the adverse event. Indeed, the need for health professionals to submit reports of adverse effects without themselves evaluating whether there was any direct connection was essential. The scheme was intended to be monitored for unusual patterns of emergence of adverse events beyond the normal occurrence of events in the general population. Therefore, it is necessary that all events are reported in order for signals of adverse events that are beyond the background rate to be detected. Failing to report a potential adverse event would be detrimental to the purpose and effectiveness of the scheme, and contribute to a false perception of safety.

In 2018, the MHRA issued guidance aimed at encouraging health professionals to make proactive use of the Yellow Card scheme noting that there had been a significant drop in reports especially among physicians. They highlighted that as few as 10% of serious adverse reactions and only 2-4% of less serious reactions were being reported [229]. A systematic review of 37 research papers spanning twelve countries shows that this was a common problem, concluding that between 85% and 95% of serious adverse drug reactions were never reported [230].

A letter published in the BMJ expressed concern over adverse effects noting that the CDC system used to collect data in the USA is passive and reports of adverse events could be as low as 1% of those that actually occurred [231]. Despite this, the author notes that the rate of adverse effects reported for COVID-19 vaccines was already almost 50 times the volume of reports associated with influenza vaccines. Evidence supporting extremely low reporting figures can be found in a study prepared for the US Department for Health and Human Services, published in 2010. The study was specifically designed to investigate reporting rates for adverse reactions to medicines [232]. It states:

...1-13% of serious events are reported to the Food and Drug Administration (FDA). Likewise, fewer than 1% of vaccine adverse events are reported.

Experts who published analysis of the risk and benefit of COVID-19 vaccination noted that adverse event reporting rates between different countries were wildly different - the Polish reporting approximately 98% fewer events than the Dutch [233]. As there is no known scientific basis for assuming that certain populations are somehow significantly more susceptible to side effects than others, the authors – Walach et al. - inferred that this was due to the veracity of the culture and mechanisms in place to ensure accurate data collection. In other words, it was how aware patients and practitioners were of the importance for reporting all suspected side effects, how seriously they took their responsibility to submit reports, and the capability and effectiveness of the infrastructure in place for report submission that affected reporting rates. The researchers, including medical experts and a data scientist, used evidence from a large-scale field study performed in Israel, alongside Dutch figures for adverse events, to compare mortality from COVID-19 with adverse events and reported deaths associated with vaccination. They defended their decision to use the Dutch data on the basis that this system was considerably more robust, and more actively engaged with, than those used in other countries. The data from this system suggested that, following vaccination, around 1 in 25 000 died and 1 in 6,250 developed severe illnesses. The shocking conclusion of the Dutch/Israeli study was that, at best, one person would die as a result of inoculation for every eight lives saved. At worst, three lives saved from COVID-19 as a result of vaccination would result in two deaths due to receipt of the vaccine. Perversely, this scenario would still fit the MHRA's appalling definition of 'safe' [234]:

> *For a medicine or vaccine to be considered safe, the expected benefits will be greater than the risk of having harmful reactions.*

Note the use of the word 'expected'. This definition means that a medicine that killed 99 people but was 'expected' to save 100 could be described as safe. It is absurd. It also ignores broader ethics. Even on the grimmest conclusions of the study that analysed the Dutch vaccine adverse events, the life for life cost of vaccination compared with non-vaccination appears mathematically justified, albeit barely - 3 saved for 2 killed. However, the study does not account for QALYS (quality adjusted life years). In other words, vaccine deaths could disproportionately affect younger people, whereas those dying from the disease are far older. Would we want to sacrifice the lives of two children or two middle-aged parents for an extra couple of years for three octogenarians? Hopefully such a question should make you feel uncomfortable because the sanctity of life should not be reduced to mere mathematics. Furthermore, the study does not account for additional risks from vaccination such as vaccine-induced viral evolution, antibody-dependent enhancement, long term chronic illness and pathologies that contribute to future death. Nor does it account for substantial natural immunity present from robust primary immune responses, or previous infection with SARS-CoV-2 or other corona viruses. As the long-term efficacy of the vaccines is not known, whether any protection provided will be long-lasting is also not accounted for.

It is possible that those protected and counted as lives saved in the short-term might actually succumb to a variant that vaccines do not protect against. It is also possible that the protection afforded by the vaccines against existing variants subsides and becomes ineffective. The unknown medium and long-term risks from vaccination and unaccounted for benefits of natural immunity may significantly alter this risk benefit ratio making vaccines more dangerous than the disease. No doubt the MHRA would not 'expect' that to be the case so such discourse would not alter their opinion over the safety of the vaccines. However, it is important not to become too bogged down in cold analysis of risk and benefit. The researchers who published the alarming cost/benefit ratios of vaccination, based on the Dutch and Israeli data, were clear that making policy judgements based on such mathematical ratios, especially for mandating or coercing people into vaccination, is a poor approach, absent of proper ethical considerations:

...one should consider the simple legal fact that a death associated with a vaccination is different in kind and legal status from a death suffered as a consequence of an incidental infection.

Vaccine proponents who do acknowledge the risks may argue that, in the case of SARS-CoV-2, the risk is worth the benefit. However, they are looking at the problem with tunnel vision, ignorant of the lack of risk in younger people, misled by a corrupt and biased testing system, and excluding the many other ways in which the effects of the disease can be effectively managed through early interventions that have largely been ignored.

It is important to note that the research by Walach et al. that revealed the potentially appalling cost to benefit of a vaccination program, based on the Dutch and Israeli data, research that was published following peer review, was later removed by the journal's editors following overwhelming criticism from establishment scientists. As a result of this pressure several members of the journal's board resigned. Objections to the paper included the suggestion that using data from vaccine injury reporting schemes was not adequately robust for use in statistical analysis. Use of the NNV (number needed to vaccinate) was also denounced. Walach et al. did not agree with the reasons given for the retraction of their paper. Objecting to the use of statistics of reported adverse events might be valid; not because they overestimate adverse events but because research clearly shows that adverse events are significantly under-reported. The causal links between these events do need further investigation, but governments and health authorities have not done this. It is true that NNV does not account for the full picture, no statistic can ever do this, but NNV is a commonly used statistic to help inform researchers and medical professionals; it has been in use for decades.

NNV will be discussed shortly in more detail. What is most remarkable about the retraction of the paper by Walach et al., is the behaviour of one the editors who resigned from the journal. They published several arguments to highlight why Walach et al.'s study was flawed. These included petty name calling, arguments against credentials, and attempts to discredit the use of NNV [235]. All attempts were made to portray vaccines in a more positive light and disallow arguments to their detriment. The emotive nature of this outburst, and lack of capacity to deal with the evidence presented, indicates significant cognitive bias and a failure to engage with the record-breaking volume of reports of serious adverse events, and deaths that have occurred globally, shortly following vaccination.

The issue of risk versus benefit, ethics and consent is especially prescient to children. Children were reported to be at extremely low risk of death following a positive COVID test and as such there is very little direct benefit in them being vaccinated. For example, during the first twelve months of the pandemic, there were just 25 deaths following a positive COVID-19 test in the under 18 age group; during the same period, 124 under 18s had committed suicide [84]. In July 2021, Professor Semple of the SAGE group said [236]:

I'm not convinced that the evidence base there is strong enough to support vaccination of children, because we don't have complete safety data for the vaccines that we would want to use.

Even the WHO were cautious at this point stating:

More evidence is needed on the use of the different COVID-19 vaccines in children to be able to make general recommendations on vaccinating children against COVID-19.

Meanwhile, the New York Times reported that several experts already believed that the risk of vaccinating children outweighed the benefit [237]. At the same time, early July 2021, the US VAERS system had counted 11 deaths in the under 18 age group following a COVID-19 vaccine [238]. The death of one 13-year-old Michigan boy - Jakob Clynick - was a rare story that actually made it into the media. He died in his sleep three days following his vaccination. Yet despite this, the vaccine propaganda had been so successful that 90% of English parents were still keen on getting their children jabbed. Reports also emerged that councils in England were 'going rogue' and vaccinating children who were not in high-risk groups, acting against government guidelines [239].

Vaccination is not the only way of tackling a virus. There are many actions that can be taken including alterations to lifestyle and diet, effective and early treatment of co-morbidities, and cultivating a healthy and loving social and family environment. There are also effective prophylactics and treatments that can reduce the seriousness of the disease, significantly lower hospitalisation rates, and lower death rates, while still facilitating the development of naturally acquired immunity.

When it came to the threat of widespread programs of vaccination for children, dissenting doctors had largely been silent, or silenced, but some did speak out. An open letter sent to the UK's MHRA, signed by dozens of medical experts including GPs, consultants, and professors, stated [240]:

The current, available evidence clearly shows that the risk versus benefit calculation does NOT support administering rushed and **experimental** *[emphasis added] COVID -19 vaccines to children, who have virtually no risk from COVID -19, yet face known and unknown risks from the vaccines.*

While this letter was aimed at protecting those under 18, more broadly it confirmed that the informed opinion of many qualified medical practitioners was; that COVID-19 vaccines were experimental in nature, that there were known risks associated with its administration, and that there may be further serious risks that were unknown.

More vociferous opposition to the global mass vaccination program came from a group of 57 experts, attached to more than 24 medical and academic institutions, who called for an immediate halt to its roll out [241]. They highlight many of the points that you may now be familiar with: that the disease could be very effectively treated; that there had been a lack of pluralistic debate about the safety, efficacy, and necessity of the vaccines; and that there were significant potential risks associated with the vaccine from known adverse reactions through to potential for long-term problems such as chronic immune disease, antibody dependent enhancement, and immune evasion. They also noted a lack of thorough animal testing and the exclusion of vulnerable groups from early trials. Of particular concern was the known effect of the spike protein on the cardiovascular system and the damage it can cause to endothelial tissue and mitochondrial function.

ii. Efficacy, Responsibility, and Mainstream Media Misinformation

Experts writing in the Lancet, raised the issue of commonplace misinformation about vaccine efficacy that was being spread via popular media [242]. They noted that vaccine efficacy was often reported in terms of relative risk reduction (RRR), ignoring other salient statistics such as absolute risk reduction (ARR), or the number of people required to be vaccinated in order to prevent one case of infection (NNV). These latter statistics are particularly sobering:

> *ARRs tend to be ignored because they give a much less impressive effect size than RRRs: 1·3% for the AstraZeneca–Oxford, 1·2% for the Moderna–NIH, 1·2% for the J&J, 0·93% for the Gamaleya, and 0·84% for the Pfizer–BioNTech vaccines.*

Critics responded with the suggestion that ARR was not a 'scientific concept' and nothing more than circumstantial information [243]. This is symptomatic of a serious issue at the heart of authoritarian technocratic thinking. Statistics based on sample populations using empirical data are necessarily circumstantial; that is, they report on a particular set of conditions within a particular time period. Statistics never describe the totality of reality, they can always be revised and disputed, and invariably they lack nuance. This does not make them irrelevant; it just means that they are subject to change and plenty of caution is needed when using any set of statistics to make sweeping decisions about policies being applied to different populations. The authors who had said that using RRR alone was misleading, responded to their critics by saying [244]:

> *Both ARR and RRR are helpful to assess trade-offs between benefits and harm, because evidence is still limited on whether or how they change across the range of individual responses and risks related to age, co-morbidities, behaviours, and level of exposure, as well as over time - with risk of COVID-19 decreasing with vaccination scale-up or altering due to virus variants.*

Indeed, not only is ARR helpful to bring perspective when reporting vaccine trial results that report RRR, but ensuring that the public are aware of ARR in additional to the more flattering RRR, provides a more balanced portrayal of risks and benefits. This helps to avoid undue coercive influence that could be exerted by focusing solely on RRR [245].

Analysis of real-world data, following a vaccination program in Israel using the Pfizer vaccine, produced an ARR of 0.46% - half that anticipated by clinical trials [242]. In this instance, this translates into a need to vaccinate 217 people in order to prevent one case of COVID-19. This does not account for future analysis of long-term data which may factor in the effects of variants that escape vaccine-induced immunity. Such variants have been mooted to be a potential reason for ongoing booster shots, hinting at the possibility of a permanent and ongoing vaccination program. The real-world data from Israel does suggest that criticism of the Pfizer study by Peter Doshi, the editor of the BMJ, who raised issues over transparency and manipulation of data may well be justified [246]. Doshi suggested that an independent analysis of Pfizer's results might well have shown that the vaccine was not as potent as claimed, potentially much less effective than the threshold required for the vaccine (or any vaccine) to be granted a fully licensed approval.

An annual vaccination program that mimics the culture of annual influenza vaccinations may well be undesirable - not just for the potential risks of vaccine-induced viral evolution and antibody dependent enhancement but also due to the high economic cost, low efficacy, and distraction from methods, other than vaccines, that can be effective in controlling and treating the disease. Outcomes from mass vaccination for respiratory viruses can be poor. For example, there is some reduction in incidence of influenza resulting from vaccination programs, but the actual benefit is low - equating to protection for just 1 person per every 100 vaccinated [247]. There is no evidence of any significant decrease in mortality [248]. The practice of such marginally effective medicine seems inconsequential to corporate profits. In 2019, the flu vaccine market was reported to be worth around $4.5 billion [249]. If vaccine manufacturers were subject to liability for their products this might be significantly reduced. However, manufacturers have been made all but immune to liability. In the USA, manufacturers are protected from taking financial responsibility for the adverse outcomes of their vaccines through law which includes: the National Childhood Vaccine Injury Act of 1986, a related 2018 court decision that de-claws individual state legislation and prevents states imposing liability, and the PREP Act [250, 251, 252].

In place of manufacturer liability, there is a national vaccine injury compensation program (NVICP). This allows claims for only the most serious categories of injury and compensation packages much lower than would typically be awarded through the courts. Between 2006 and 2018, a period in which over 3.7 billion vaccines were administered in the US, there were 4,444 claims brought to the NVICP for injuries sustained as a result of influenza vaccines [253]. 3,783 were successful. In total, 7,633 injuries were alleged to have been caused by 31 different types of vaccine. Within the EU, liability for vaccine-induced injury is a little more complex but liability exclusion clauses are said to have been negotiated by the manufacturers of SARS-CoV-2 vaccines, meaning the member states or the European Commission will be responsible for dealing with any claims arising from vaccine-injured parties [254].

Vaccine manufacturers also avoid liability in the UK, which has a similar government-mediated vaccine damage payment scheme to the USA. Late in 2020, COVID-19 vaccines were added to this scheme prior to their release. As of 2021, the maximum payout in the UK is limited to £120 000. This can only be claimed if the injured party has suffered a minimum of 60% disability and, if paid, can adversely affect other payments for benefits and entitlements [255]. If a vaccine-caused injury only results in 50% disability - tough - you get nothing. For most vaccines, there are also additional clauses to restrict claimants by age - the majority of vaccines covered require you to be aged 18 or under when the injury occurs. So, if you are completely disabled following a tetanus vaccine at the age of 19, or a meningitis vaccine at the age of 30 - tough - you get nothing. This level of compensation and standard of measuring injury is significantly lower than might be awarded through British courts if injured parties were not blocked from bringing claims against the product manufacturers. Since the scheme was set up in 1979, the UK government has paid out just 941 out of 6352 claims brought [256]. It is not clear how many people are aware of the scheme's existence. Nor is it clear whether people are aware of the full dangers vaccines can present.

Serious harm caused by the COVID-19 vaccines was anticipated. UK government guidance for medical practitioners administering SARS-CoV-2 vaccines warned of at least a dozen potential adverse effects and included advice about the need to be aware of, and prepared to respond to, the possibility of anaphylaxis [257]. These dangers may be comparatively low, but they can be life-changing and sometimes fatal. Odds of a serious anaphylactic shock capable of causing death were estimated to be around 1 in 1 million in pre-covid-19 vaccines [258]. This appears to be a very conservative estimate (by orders of magnitude when compared with data of reported SARS-CoV-2 vaccine side effects) but it is still around 18 times more likely than winning the UK lottery jackpot. It could be you? To date no detailed, evidence-based, analysis of the hundreds and thousands of side effects reported to the MHRA has been made public. It does appear likely that far more people have been affected than one per million. Cursory mention of background incidence rates and attribution of coincidence is not a satisfactory approach. Also, anaphylaxis is only one of many immune system complications that may arise. Others identified by experts include [259]:

...local and systemic inflammatory responses, the bio-distribution and persistence of the induced immunogen expression, possible development of auto-reactive antibodies, and toxic effects of any non-native nucleotides and delivery system components.

Risks for vaccine-injury are difficult to predict. For example, an influenza vaccine launched in Australia in 2010 was expected to be safe. However, the government were forced to halt the program for the under 5s when reports indicated that around 1 in 110 children were having seizures following vaccination [260]. The final figure for incidence of seizures was suggested to be closer to 1 in 200 children. The convulsions were blamed on a heightened immune response caused by too many viral ingredients being included in the jab [261]. This example illustrates how irresponsible it is to claim that a novel vaccine is safe. The reason the Australian vaccine affected some children and not others is still not known. This is a key point about using statistics to predict risk. What is tacit, but not often admitted is that the person-specific interaction - what is actually going on - is simply not understood. In reality, the chance of adverse effects in the victim is 100% and for the unaffected 0%. Something notable about the case of the halted program of flu vaccination in Australia was that the manufacturer performed studies for several years *after* the incident in order to investigate what caused the children to have seizures. Their intention was to use that information to refine production for future use. This is clear evidence that the vaccine that was initially deployed was, in reality, experimental.

There is a clear need to move beyond a banal binary pro-vax / anti-vax debate and understand that for all the potential good they were hoped to do, there were genuine, scientifically-based, concerns about the detrimental effects of vaccines in general and especially about SARS-CoV-2 vaccines. Indeed, Bill Gates suggested that a severe adverse reaction to COVID-19 vaccines could occur in approximately 1 in 10 000 people (0.01%) - an issue he was highlighting because of the risk of compensation claims [262]:

> *...governments will have to be involved because there will be some risk and indemnification needed...*

Members of the fact-checking Stasi claimed he meant side effects in general and the 1 in 10 000 figure was purely hypothetical. By this they presumably mean fabricated or not evidence-based? If that were the case, would you not expect them to be leading a public outcry over such a prominent, and powerfully vocal, vaccine-promoting activist just making statistics up on the spot? Either way, the claim that Gates might have been referring to minor adverse effects occurring in 1 in 10 000 people is demonstrably incorrect. Initial trials showed high levels of minor adverse effects. For example, in Moderna trials, up to 70% who received the vaccine reported symptoms such as fatigue; more than 1% reported serious adverse effects [263].

As the vaccination program was rolled out, adverse effects became such a common concern that some sections of the popular media began to promote them as a good thing [264]. An NHS consultant, writing about concerns over mandatory vaccination did not agree [265]:

...what I am currently struggling with is the failure to report the reality of the morbidity caused by our current vaccination program within the health service and staff population. The levels of sickness after vaccination is unprecedented and staff are getting very sick and some with neurological symptoms which is having a huge impact on the health service function.

In the same letter, the consultant, a person who had worked in front-line delivery of COVID-19 hospital services, went on to say:

Mandatory vaccination in this instance [for NHS staff] is stupid, unethical and irresponsible...

Only a few weeks after it was published, the BMJ made the rare move of censoring this letter and removing it from their website [266]. The reason they gave was not because of the content of the letter itself but because other people were misrepresenting what it said. As should be obvious to any reasonable person, access to the original letter would be absolutely essential to prove misrepresentation. Imagine if we banned every publication because some other party misinterpreted or misrepresented what it said? There would simply be no books, newspapers, magazines, or scientific publications allowed anywhere. You could get something somebody else wrote banned simply by writing an inaccurate blog article about it. This is utterly absurd, but indicative of the sort of irrational, cult-like, book-burning mindset that has been increasingly imposed by the mechanisms of governance and control that have emerged under the veil of the corona virus pandemic. Of course, there is only one reason the BMJ banned Polyakova's letter - they (possibly under significant external pressure) did not want people to read it.

Such censorship does not encourage reasonable and rational discussion or debate. It only acts as an assertion of political authority and force of will, sending a clear signal that it is power and authority that are shaping dominant narratives and not calm reason or scientific logic. The use of such political censorship acts to avoid themes of discussion becoming more widespread and open to investigation. This is the opposite of what science is and what scientists should be doing. It is particularly problematic when an experimental drug is being deployed against a novel disease on such a wide scale.

According to the repetitive, banal, child-like mantra of the vaccine cult, SARS-CoV-2 vaccines are 'safe and effective'. If they were safe, the manufacturers would have no need to seek to evade liability through legislation or contract clauses for damage caused by their products. They do so because vaccines are not *completely* safe. Nor are they *fully* effective. In fact, the history of vaccines is littered with incidents that would, quite understandably, cause people to feel a little cautious about taking them despite their proven efficacy in reducing or eliminating the incidence of many diseases. One example is a decades-long controversy about contaminated polio vaccines that were administered during the late 1950s. Evidence was found that the vaccines had somehow been contaminated with SV40 - a simian vacuolating DNA virus. SV40 is associated with a risk of causing cancer [267]. Analysis of vaccinated populations suggested that there was enhanced incidence of cancer in those who had been vaccinated - 98 million people in total [268]. It is difficult for analysts to conclude definitively how many people may have been affected. The vaccine used deactivated polio virus and the deactivation process should also have deactivated the SV40, but the process failed. How many and who got inoculated with what is not clear. However, the evidence is compelling and what is clear is that there has been some effect causing increased incidence of cancers amongst the vaccinated population. In 2006, a consultant for pharmaceutical companies presented an argument that there was no evidence that SV40 caused cancer. His intention was seemingly to dispel concerns associated with vaccines (although it is notable, and laudable, that he did make robust suggestions for improving vaccine development to help promote trust in the technology) [269]. However, robust analysis shows firm evidence for a link between SV40 and cancer, particularly bone cancer [270, 271, 272]. Decades later, scientists are still investigating the link and potential causal mechanisms.

Polio vaccines have proved controversial for other reasons too. There is no question that global vaccination programs appear to have been successful in contributing to a massive reduction in the disease. However, there are still numerous polio cases being reported in Pakistan, India, and some countries in Africa. Often, they are actually caused by the vaccine, but attempts are made to keep such incidents out of the public eye [273, 274]. In November 2019, Edna Mohamed reported in the Guardian [275]:

...more children are now being paralysed by vaccine-derived viruses than those infected by viruses in the wild, according to global health numbers.

Analysis of rates of non-polio acute flaccid paralysis in India, which were suspiciously higher than expected, show an extremely strong statistical relationship with rates of oral polio vaccination [277]. The authors who made this discovery suggest that as many as 490 000 cases of paralysis may have been caused by polio vaccine programs during the period 2000-2017. They recommended reducing the extent of the vaccination program. Despite this, and the fact that many of those targeted by vaccine programs lack access to the most basic human health needs, such as fresh drinking water and effective sewer systems, international aid agencies continue to prioritise vaccination programs [276]. Oral polio vaccines are cheap and easy to administer. However, they have also caused infections and mutations of the disease leading to the absurd situation that most vaccines are now administered to protect populations from infection caused by mutated disease that has arisen from previous vaccination programs [274]. In other words, there is a reservoir of people who are incubating polio variants following vaccine programs. Therefore, it would seem historically short-sighted to herald the permanent success of polio vaccines. If a virulent mutation were to arise in a population who were suddenly no longer able to access vaccines, perhaps due to natural disaster or conflict, there could be an epidemic. The potential for an unanticipated mutation that proves to be vaccine resistant leading to an epidemic cannot be eliminated either. Evolution can produce surprises, suddenly, and unexpectedly.

Possibly the most notorious incident involving polio vaccines was the Cutter incident in the USA [278]. This involved polio vaccines that directly caused 40 000 polio infections resulting in 200 paralysed children, and 10 deaths. The incident became infamous because of a legal judgement arising from claims made for compensation for vaccine injury. The manufacturer, Cutter, had followed all published guidelines in the manufacture of the vaccine and so was not found to have acted negligently yet was still held liable for damages because the product did not match the manufacturer's claim that it was 'safe and effective'. This seems to be perfectly understandable. If someone tells you something is safe and effective, yet it is ineffective, and in some cases, extremely dangerous, surely there should be serious consequences? The pharmaceutical industry was so concerned about the future economic viability of vaccines that they lobbied government to address the issue of liability. The incident led to the legal changes that exonerated manufacturers from liability and instituted the government-backed vaccine injury compensation program and similar programs in other countries. Effectively this means that manufacturers can continue to claim that vaccines are 'safe and effective' without concern about liability arising from an event similar to, or worse than, the Cutter incident. Some may believe this was the right thing to do in view of the benefits that vaccines are said to bring. However, an alternative view may be that this has led vaccine science astray from the thorough, longitudinal studies and due diligence in manufacture and administration, that could have led to more effective risk management, and a safer, more effective, vaccine industry.

Vaccine producers might prefer to avoid liability but not all countries have acquiesced to demands to instantiate sweeping schemes such as those in the UK and USA which liberate vaccine makers from liability for their products. For example, the Brazilian government were astounded by the demands made by Pfizer executives during contract negotiations over the supply of SARS-CoV-2 vaccines and accused them of bullying the country. Pfizer were insisting that Brazil set up a government-backed indemnity scheme as a fund to cover claims following adverse effects from vaccine administration [279]. To cover the full extent of potential liabilities, Pfizer were demanding that this fund be backed up by government assets including military bases and embassy buildings. They threatened to refuse to supply any vaccines if Brazil did not meet their demands. There is some suggestion other countries may also have been subject to such coercion, but confidentiality agreements may prevent public disclosure.

By August of 2021, data from Public Health England and analysis by SAGE concluded that vaccinated people infected with COVID-19 were found to be carrying the same viral load and therefore had the same potential for spreading the virus to others as unvaccinated people did [280]. What they did not admit was that vaccinated people were more likely to form an environment capable of producing more virulent and deadly strains. This tacit admission that vaccination had failed was accompanied by an alternative suggestion for ending the COVID-19 crisis - to stop testing people who were not sick and to stop counting 'cases'.

iii. Acute and Chronic Heart, Blood, and Circulatory Problems

Of the many reported post-vaccination adverse effects, blood clots were one of the few that received some coverage in the popular media. Due to the prevalence of the issue, it would have been difficult to ignore. In March 2021, Norwegian scientists sparked controversy when they declared that the vaccine was the only viable causal explanation for the occurrence of blood clots in three health workers shortly after they had been injected with the AstraZeneca vaccine [281]. One of the workers later died. Some experts, including June Raine of the UK's MHRA, dismissed the event, and many others like it, as a coincidence. Unfortunately, the MHRA did not, and still have not, published any evidence-based review showing how they arrived at that conclusion. It appears that they expected their word to be taken as fact without question. By contrast, researchers in Germany who took the issue seriously found that there appeared to be an immune-induced response in the blood that caused clotting on the brain leading to blocked blood flows - a condition known as thrombosis [282]. The effect is similar to the clotting occurring when a wound heals. Ordinarily this wouldn't happen with internal blood flows, but the vaccine was found to be associated with the activation of blood platelets causing them in some cases to form clots.

Shortly after the German research connecting vaccines and blood clots had been made public, the MHRA admitted that there were dozens of reported cases of thrombosis in the UK. Most were brain clots and at least seven people had died [283]. However, they insisted that the events were rare and continued to use the word 'safe' to describe the vaccine. By early April 2021, the head of the European Medicines Agency declared that there was a clear link between the AstraZeneca vaccine and blood clotting, but they did not fully understand the mechanism at that point [284]. The MHRA then confessed that, by that point, 19 people had died due to clots, including three people under the age of 30 [285]. In mid-April 2021, Denmark became the first country to stop the rollout of the AstraZeneca vaccine completely. Their decision was made after they found that vaccine-associated blood clots had killed at least one person and appeared to affect 1 in 40 000 people - a much higher number than expected. The BBC reported the issue, but in an addendum to their report they referred to the viral spike protein, the one the body produced following vaccination, as 'harmless' [286]. This is a scientifically inaccurate piece of propaganda aimed at discouraging scepticism over vaccine safety; as shall be shown shortly, the spike protein is far from harmless.

The UK had completely missed early warnings over a link between clots and the AstraZeneca vaccine. It appeared the reason for this was that the MHRA was using an automated monitoring system deploying algorithms in a hastily constructed computer program [287]. It seems nobody was checking the data; everything was being left to software. Who coded it is unclear and no independent team has been given access to audit the program to ensure it is both medically and computationally accurate.

Stories of serious and deadly blood clots occurring following vaccination continued to surface. These included a serious illness for Princess Michael of Kent, the death of BBC Radio Presenter Lisa Shaw, the death of a British model - Leah Sinclair - who was living in Cyprus, the death of 47-year-old mum of three Lucy Taberer, and the death of 43 year-old mum Tanya Smith [288, 289, 290, 291, 292]. In July, Vikki Spit, the partner of a man who died in excruciating pain from blood clots on the brain following an AstraZeneca vaccine, pleaded with people to reject being 'fobbed off'. She was concerned that medical personnel were being inattentive to potential links between the presentation of medical symptoms and links with serious adverse effects caused by the vaccines [293].

Such cognitive blind spots become inevitable in a population that is subject to constant propaganda that downplays and dismisses the bad side of vaccines. They affect medical professionals and patients alike. Charlotte Wright, the wife of a UK man who had died due to vaccine side effects, described how she had been in denial about the link for a long time because both her and her recently deceased 32-year-old husband were so enthusiastic about getting vaccinated [294]. Had the link not been medically confirmed it is unlikely she would have entertained the idea. Once she had come to terms with the fact that her young and healthy husband had been killed by a vaccine, Charlotte Wright began to campaign for an overhaul of the compensation scheme for UK vaccine injuries and expressed dismay at the lack of help and support for the vaccine victims and their families.

As a result of mounting clot-related deaths (over 60 confirmed by June 2021) plus the number of non-fatal clots occurring following use of the AstraZeneca vaccine, the MHRA reluctantly restricted its use in the under 40s. Both AstraZeneca and Johnson and Johnson - whose vaccine had also been causing clots - said they were working on ways of reducing the risk [295]. Remember, just months earlier the MHRA, in reliance on their algorithms, had said there was no safety issue. In July 2021, data analysis by scientists suggested that the Pfizer vaccine, previously presumed safer, appeared to have an equal or greater risk of causing clots than the AstraZeneca vaccine [296]. Blood clots were not the only cardiovascular problems associated with the vaccines. In June 2021, a 13-year-old boy from Michigan who was claimed to have been otherwise healthy, died from an enlarged heart three days following receipt of a Pfizer injection [297]. In a particularly tragic case, a 45-year-old woman from Baltimore, Maryland, vaccinated in response to a mandate imposed upon her as a condition of employment, died following an adverse vaccine reaction which caused swelling on the brain and heart problems [298].

Links to vaccination and myocarditis were investigated by researchers who studied a cohort of military personnel. They found 23 personnel, people who had been extremely fit and healthy, went on to develop myocarditis within 4 days of receiving a COVID-19 vaccine [299]. No other cause could be identified. Notably, 20 of the cases occurred following the second vaccination dose. The researchers concluded that prior exposure was a significant factor in the hypersensitivity response and indicated that people who have recovered from a prior COVID-19 infection would be at much greater risk of developing myocarditis in response to vaccination.

A group of researchers who investigated the potential causal connection between SARS-CoV-2 and heart problems (in this instance myocardial hypertrophy) concluded that the S1 subunit of the spike protein was capable of harming heart cells by triggering their innate immune response [300]. In August 2021, the US CDC released an interim report into adverse events following COVID-19 vaccination in children aged 12-17 [301]. The most notable finding was a high prevalence of myocarditis; figures suggested it affected around 1 in 22 000 children. The cause of myocarditis is likely to be an auto-immune response induced by the vaccine. Many of those who suffer myocarditis and survive in the short-term will have a reduced life expectancy with some dying from heart complications in the years following the initial myocarditis event [302].

Thrombocytopenia is another pathology that has commonly occurred following vaccination. The condition refers to a low blood platelet count. Blood platelets are essential to help blood form clots; a lack of platelets can lead to spontaneous and/or excessive bleeding, including inducement of large areas of bruising under the skin. While this may seem to be the opposite of blood clotting, the two events - clot formation and low platelet counts, sometimes accompanied by excessive bleeding, are associated. The condition is called TTS - thrombosis with thrombocytopenia syndrome - and is known to be caused by certain vaccines including the AstraZeneca vaccine and the Johnson and Johnson vaccine which have an adenovirus-based vector [303]. Indeed, it has been known for many years that adenovirus-based vaccines can cause thrombocytopenia - a paper released in 2003 confirmed that inoculation with replication-incompetent adenovirus was clearly associated with the induction of low platelet counts [304]. The effect was correlative with dose.

The use of adenovirus vectors for the delivery of gene therapy products (which is really what the DNA and mRNA-based vaccines are) was confirmed as a serious safety issue in 2007 due to the effects on blood platelet counts; evidence of endothelial activation was also found [305]. Endothelial activation is an inflammatory state of the tissue that lines blood cells and can increase the likelihood of coagulation (blood clotting). Experts who examined the mechanism of adenovirus-based DNA COVID-19 vaccines found that they were significantly more likely to induce inflammatory responses in endothelial tissue, especially following a second dose, than mRNA vaccines [306]. They specifically identified an issue with events that occurred while the cell was producing proteins from the RNA (that had been created from the injected DNA). Problematic variations of the spike protein were produced provoking a pathogenic autoimmune response. The researchers called this vaccine-induced COVID-19 mimicry syndrome because the vaccines were effectively creating a disease comparable with COVID-19 itself. With respect to this issue, they confirmed that the DNA sequences used by AstraZeneca appeared to be far more problematic than those used in the Johnson and Johnson vaccine and that vaccine manufacturers needed to work harder on the complexities of how their products worked in order to make them safer.

Thrombocytopenia is not solely associated with adenovirus-based vaccines. It has also been linked with measles vaccines, including the MMR vaccine. A study that investigated reports from the VAERS (Vaccine Adverse Event Reporting System) in the US confirmed that serious thrombocytopenia, including deaths associated with gastrointestinal damage and sepsis, was associated with measles vaccines [307]. The general incidence was low (around 1 in 30 000), but the researchers did suggest that caution should be advised in patients who may have a propensity for developing thrombocytopenia. However, most physicians may lack knowledge about the potential for novel therapies to induce thrombotic events. In 2015, the publication of a detailed meta-analysis about physicians knowledge of treatment-induced thrombotic events, revealed that there was serious under-reporting of both venous and arterial thrombosis in randomised control trials, the majority of which had not even bothered to include the conditions when reporting on product safety [308]. The implications are stark. If physicians are not even aware of the possibility of a connection, then making a link between a treatment and an ensuing medical condition becomes highly unlikely. The true extent of such links is then lost in the darkness of the medical profession's collective cognitive blind spot.

There has been much debate and uncertainty about what is causing the side effects attributed to the vaccines, especially with regard to thrombocytopenia and other heart and circulatory problems. Autoimmune responses were implicated and appear to be exacerbated by repeat exposure to proteins present in the virus and produced as a consequence of vaccination. What is clear, is that the highly active scientific debate only reinforces the view that, regardless of any official or legal label attached to them, the vaccines being administered in 2020 and 2021 were very much experimental.

<u>iv. Temporary Drop in Immune Function</u>

Like most vaccines, it was known that COVID-19 vaccines could cause a temporary but notable drop in the efficacy of the immune system for a period of up to a week following inoculation. For reasonably healthy people this may be of small consequence but for those most susceptible to the virus, this indicated a serious additional risk. If vaccine recipients were already carrying the virus but had yet to show symptoms, or if they picked up an infection either from SARS-CoV-2, influenza, or some other infectious disease soon after their vaccination, then their ability to fight these additional challenges in the post-inoculation period would be significantly diminished. This could be especially salient for the elderly, people who have had organ transplants, and people with poorly functioning immune systems; a problematic fact when coupled with evidence that vaccines may be completely ineffective for some people within these groups [309]. It would make inoculation all risk and no benefit. One way of handling the risk of exposure during the vaccination process would have been to test people pre-vaccine to ensure they were not already carrying the disease. Another would have been to test people at the same time as they received their vaccine so that vaccination centres with huge throughputs of people could be monitored in case they became the potential source of infection for vulnerable persons. None of this was done. There is evidence that suggests people with symptomatic disease were avoiding tests and attending vaccine centres [310].

Numerous stories have emerged where lethal outbreaks of disease were reported following a program of vaccination. Cambodia was a nation that had seen comparatively

86

low impact from infection and zero deaths before it commenced its national vaccine program toward the end of February 2021 [311]. Within a month, cases in the nation had doubled - the spike in cases commencing ten days after the vaccine program was rolled out [312]. Reports also emerged from care homes that suddenly experienced unexplained deaths, and sometimes lethal outbreaks of COVID-19, after administering vaccines to residents; such incidents were reported in the UK, Germany, Norway, and Canada [313, 314, 315, 316]. Some have speculated about a direct link with the vaccine as the potential cause. However, another potential explanation is that weakening the immune systems of a cohort of vulnerable people, combined with the presence of medical staff who were entering and leaving different places regularly, might have created a perfect opportunity for opportunist pathogenic infection to take hold, replicate and spread.

In a study published by the Coronavirus Clinical Characterisation Consortium, it was shown that the majority of people who had been vaccinated, but were later admitted to hospital for treatment for COVID-19, had been infected around the time of vaccination [317]. An example of further evidence for the risk of infection occurring during the vaccination procedure comes from reports that a testing centre in Cardiff, Wales, was found to have been staffed by several people who tested positive for COVID-19 after assisting in the vaccination process [318]. Aside from the immediate risk of short-term effects and increased risk of infection due to lowered immune system function, other potential undesirable consequences of vaccination are more complex and some could take a much longer period to emerge.

<u>v. Antibody Dependent Enhancement</u>

In 2018, the researchers Smatti et al. discussed several studies involving corona viruses [319]. They drew attention to evidence of antibody-dependent enhancement (ADE) – a mechanism which enables a virus to become more effective at penetrating cells by harnessing antibodies which have failed to neutralise it. The ordinary mechanism of an antibody-enabled immune response would be for the antibody to attach to the virus and act as a signal and means of entry into cells (lymphocytes) which enclose the virus and then proceed to break it down, rendering it harmless. However, through ADE, viruses can develop the ability to use this process by using the antibody as a trojan horse to enable access to the cell. The immune cell fails to break the virus down once it is inside. Instead, the virus hi-jacks the cell and uses it as a virus factory. It is clear that there were good grounds for acknowledging the very real risk of ADE and those developing SARS-CoV-2 vaccines would have been wise to be thorough in their trials to ensure they were not introducing something that, in time, could potentially make a disease outbreak worse or cause serious complications for some of those who have been vaccinated. To do this properly would have taken considerable time. However, there was a dearth of clinical studies that investigated ADE in SARS-CoV patients [319].

Concern about ADE was echoed in an article that appeared in the journal 'Nature' in June of 2020. The authors made a strong argument that full exploration of potential risks from ADE must be investigated during SARS-CoV-2 vaccine development [320]. However, shortly afterwards, another paper was published in Nature explaining that there was in fact no reliable way of predicting the risk for ADE in humans, nor were there reliable clinical indicators that could assist in differentiating severe infection from an illness severely exacerbated by antibody dependent enhancement [321]. This implies that it is near impossible to calculate the risk of ADE without prolonged and intense study requiring the use of human subjects. If ADE occurred on a significant scale, the effects could easily be attributed to another cause such as a new variant, especially if doctors were not aware of the risk of ADE and had no means by which to identify it. ADE associated with prior exposure to other forms of corona virus in elderly populations has also been proposed as one of the potential factors causing higher death rates within that demographic [322]. In January 2021, a further article appeared in the journal 'Cell Death and Differentiation', a journal published by Nature, that supported concerns about ADE. The authors highlighted several areas of uncertainty relating to the novel corona virus vaccines including: a lack of evidence for long-term protection, uncertainty as to vaccine efficacy in vulnerable groups, and a lack of understanding about long-term risks [323]:

...the time required to evaluate the dangers and risks that may arise from a new vaccine must be included in its development. In some cases, vaccines prepared against other corona viruses or other viruses have worsened the disease and have induced T helper 2-type immunopathology.

As already mentioned, a serious complication in trying to understand and study the effects of ADE is that there is no easy or reliable way of telling if any given patient is suffering due to a serious viral infection or due to an infection that has been seriously exacerbated by ADE [321]. The apparent lack of concern shown by those performing clinical trials for COVID-19 vaccines is disconcerting. A review published in Nature in October of 2020 warned that there was a real possibility that ADE could occur with SARS-CoV-2 [324]. The Nature article also confirmed that there was an additional danger with non-antibody related enhanced respiratory disease (known as ERD) - effectively similar to ADE in the sense that an infection could be made far more severe as a result of immune-responses that were over-stimulated as a result of inoculation. Experts in medical ethics who performed a thorough review of the literature concerning ADE within the context of the ethics of disclosure applied to SARS-CoV-2 vaccine trials concluded [325]:

...vaccines designed empirically using the traditional approach (consisting of the unmodified or minimally modified corona virus viral spike to elicit neutralising antibodies), be they composed of protein, viral vector, DNA or RNA and irrespective of delivery method, may worsen COVID-19 disease via antibody-dependent enhancement (ADE). This risk is sufficiently obscured in clinical trial protocols and consent forms for ongoing COVID-19 vaccine trials that adequate patient comprehension of this risk is unlikely to occur, obviating truly informed consent by subjects in these trials.

If a lack of consent was an issue in clinical trials, then it would certainly have been pertinent to the roll out of vaccines to the general public. Early, short-term animal studies did suggest low risk from ADE in vaccines used in trials, including the AstraZeneca vaccine [326, 327].

However, these conclusions were drawn from extremely small populations with weak statistical certainty; they did not examine ADE directly but observed that the animals experimented upon predominantly produced T_H1 cells rather than T_H2 cells - T_H2 cells usually being associated with ADE. Data from the ZOE Covid symptom study analysed in May 2021, suggested that those who had been exposed to the virus, and then later received a vaccination, were twice as likely to experience adverse reactions – a likely sign of immunopathology [328].

<u>vi. Pathogenic Priming and Autoimmunity</u>

A notably succinct and informative review paper was published on the 9th of April 2020, in the Journal of Translational Immunity, an Elsevier publication. It was titled, 'Pathogenic priming likely contributes to serious and critical illness and mortality in COVID-19 via autoimmunity'. The author – Dr James Lyons-Weiler – has previously acted as an expert witness in vaccine injury cases held by the National Vaccine Injury Program in the USA [329]. In his article, Lyons-Weiler discusses the findings of autopsies on Chinese patients who had died with COVID-19. They found lung scarring associated with autoimmune pathology. This was evidence of serious and sometimes fatal lung damage caused by the patient's immune systems attacking their own lung tissue. Lyons-Weiler proceeds to discuss several interesting research papers dating back as far as 2004. These papers contained evidence from experiments in which animals vaccinated with a corona virus (SARS-CoV or MERS-CoV) were later exposed to the same disease, or a similar one, to that with which they had been vaccinated. This is called a 'challenge' as it challenges the organism's immune response to the pathogen and is designed to test the efficacy of the vaccine. The results showed that serious complications occurred as a result of what is normally termed 'immune enhancement'. Lyons-Weiler prefers to refer to this using the less euphemistic term 'pathogenic priming'. The studies showed that once the animals' immune systems had been primed by an initial exposure to viral proteins through inoculation, the immune system response was so dramatic when exposed to the real virus that it proved to have disastrous effects. Many animals developed serious conditions such as hepatitis and lung damage, and some died. These studies were of particular concern to the COVID-19 outbreak because the cause of death for many patients was pneumonia-type symptoms in the lungs associated with a 'cytokine storm'.

The cytokine storm is a dramatic, and damaging, immune response. Therefore, there could potentially be a significant risk of harm when a person's immune system is subject to multiple exposures to the SARS-CoV-2 viral proteins. Such repeat exposure may lead to an over-reactive response with serious symptoms and potentially chronic or fatal consequences for some people. Examples of how this additional risk could be created include: catching the disease and recovering followed by a later vaccination; receiving a vaccination followed by a later exposure to the virus; having two or more vaccinations. The more incidents of vaccination and/or exposure to the virus, or similar viruses, the more enhanced this risk might become (for *some* people).

The mechanism for pathogenic priming is known and well explained in Lyons-Weiler's paper. Medical science recognises a large number of known immunogenic peptides – these are peptides that have been shown to cause an immune response and are capable of sensitising the immune system in a way that, for some individuals, could cause allergenic type responses. (Amino acids are the building blocks of peptides, peptides are the building blocks of proteins, and proteins are the building blocks of life.) Mechanisms for how these autoimmune responses could occur include epitope spreading, molecular mimicry, cryptic antigen, and bystander activation; these are ways in which the immune system comes to recognise non-pathogenic elements - such as elements of our own body - as pathogens that need to be attacked. The H1N1 outbreak of 2009 and subsequent global vaccination programs produced evidence for such a causal link with vaccines [330]. Following mass vaccination programs against H1N1, there was a significant increase in cases of narcolepsy in Europe and China within the vaccinated population. The suggested mechanism was linked to a similarity between an influenza surface protein and a neuropeptide secreted by the hypothalamus that is involved in the modulation of sleep function.

The same H1N1 vaccine was associated with an increased risk for Guillain-Barre Syndrome (GBS), as was the rushed and poorly researched 1976 swine flu vaccine [330]. The rollout of the 1976 swine flu vaccine was based on the alarming prediction that a pandemic could occur, mirroring that of the 1918 Spanish flu. However, the inoculations were halted due to hundreds of cases of GBS and a handful of deaths - a time when the principle of 'do no harm' appeared to have some meaning [331]. Despite vaccines being withdrawn, no pandemic occurred. GBS is a rare condition in which the immune system attacks nerve tissue leading to varying degrees of numbness, tingling, loss of limb control, and paralysis. Scientific debate concerning the emergence of serious and debilitating autoimmune disorders following vaccination has been ongoing for decades [330].

Autoimmunity can also cause or trigger mental illness, and there are proven links between autoimmunity and vaccines, although the full causal mechanisms and extent of the issue remain highly controversial. For example, statistically significant temporal correlation between vaccination and psychiatric disorders (notably anxiety) was found in a study conducted by researchers at Yale university [332]. The authors drew from prior published research to suggest brain inflammation linked to autoimmunity as a possible causative factor, but noted additional large-scale studies were required to study the matter further. Commenting on the publication, Yale immunopathologist Professor John Rose suggested that there may not be a direct biological cause between vaccination and mental illness, but instead offered the explanation that the trauma of the inoculation process may be the trigger [333]. However, the only evidence he offered in support of this idea was his own personal anecdote of having been given a polio vaccine - he offered no other tangible evidence that would support his theory. Professor Rose was basically rejecting the results of published research, based on supporting empirical data, by using his own personal anecdote because he could not accept the idea that vaccines might cause brain inflammation; the consequent symptom of such inflammation being mental illness. This illustrates how dogma and assumptions can influence the thought process of trained scientists. Such bias is illustrative of the obstacles that exist in making progress in the research of such issues. Notably,

Professor Rose was reported to have declared confidence in the safety of vaccines due to the thorough checks and procedures that went into product development:

> *Rose, who developed a vaccine template that was used for the development of the current Ebola vaccine, said he trusts the current process of drug development to establish safety measures for vaccines. On average, **a vaccine takes 15–20 years to be fully approved** [emphasis added], Rose said.*

Contrast that with the amount of time spent on producing the novel SARS-CoV-2 vaccines.

Studying the adverse effects caused by vaccines is not just difficult due to the received dogma of large parts of the biomedical science community. The complexity of the causal processes involved expose how much is not known about human biology - particularly with regard to the immune system, autoimmunity, epigenetics, and the implications of genetic specificity (how some people can be affected but not others). Additionally, there are a plethora of environmental factors which are heterogeneous across populations and through time: reactions are different for different people in different places at different times of their life. A vaccine that is safe and effective for one person may not be for another. In a small number of cases, it might kill or permanently disable them. One size does not fit all.

Limitations in funding for bench research mean that many researchers make use of advances in computer software to perform investigations that would otherwise be impossible. This is called 'in-silico' research (meaning it has taken place on a computer). Indeed, much research contributing to the construction of the SARS-CoV-2 genome, testing procedures, and vaccine development was done in this way. Researcher, Lyons-Weiler, also made use of advances in the area. When he analysed some of the proteins understood to form part of the structure of the SARS-CoV-2 virus, he found that over 2/3 contained known immunogenic peptides. 1/3 of them were known to have enough similarity to proteins in the human adaptive immune system to have potential to cause disease [329]. Furthermore, the spike protein was identified as the worst potential offender for causing complications. This was an early indication that there existed a realistic danger of an autoimmune response being triggered by a COVID-19 vaccine or by exposure to the virus itself. However, there is an important difference. Contracting a virus naturally means that it must enter the body from the outside. This means it will encounter numerous obstacles, including physical barriers and the firewall created by the primary (non-specific) immune response. Inoculation bypasses these protections and puts the immune-provoking material directly into deeper tissues via a small injury. Also, unlike the wild virus, all vaccines contain a host of other potentially immunogenic ingredients that are foreign to our internal tissues and organs; some included in SARS-CoV-2 vaccines are entirely novel and have never been used in human vaccines before. Data on their full effects including pharmacokinetics and toxicity, including genotoxicity, is poor or entirely absent for many of them.

A further complication with SARS-CoV-2 is that the S1 subunit of the spike protein is able to cross the blood-brain barrier and very rapidly enter neurological tissue [334]. The spike protein has been evidenced to have deleterious effects on brain barrier function [335]. It may also cause microvascular injury which has been linked to similar chronic health issues connected with the 'long-covid' phenomena, increasing the long-term risk of neurological deterioration including mental illness, memory dysfunction, Parkinson's, Alzheimer's disease, and other conditions connected with neuroinflammation [459]. This has implications beyond the direct adverse effects of the vaccine as the brain barrier helps protect the brain against other pathogenic viruses, bacteria, and fungi, as well as from the entry of toxins and pollutants that may be present in the blood. If the functioning of the usual barrier to entry is disrupted and other pollutants enter the delicate brain tissues, they could invoke or exacerbate long-term adverse consequences.

In his conclusion, Lyons-Weiler did not make hysterical arguments for banning vaccines. Instead he suggested that research into potential COVID-19 vaccines should ensure thorough animal testing is carried out to assess risks from potential autoimmune complications. Such research would have needed to examine the full spectrum of potential complications and observe effects on the lungs, the kidneys, the liver, and the brain. Viral neuroimmunopathology is a serious issue which can lead to impaired immunity. It makes a patient more susceptible to pathogens, encephalitis, and other long-term neurological disease including demyelination - where the nerve cell sheath is degraded causing serious dysfunction of the nervous system [336].

Lyons-Weiler's concerns were not unique. Scientists have been trying to develop corona virus vaccines for a long time. As early as 2012 another published, peer-reviewed, research paper authored by Tseng et al. forewarned [337]:

Caution in proceeding to application of a SARS-CoV vaccine in humans is indicated.

The authors noted that studies could find such vaccines to be safe but only when they focused on short-term risk. Here, they raised concerns for a similar reason to those set out by Lyons-Weiler: immunopathology of the lung from an exposure to the wild virus some time following vaccination. Of further concern is research published in the Proceedings of the National Academy of Sciences that provides evidence for the possibility that viral fragments of SARS-CoV-2 RNA can be reverse transcribed into the human genome with potential for continuous, permanent expression of viral RNA [338]. The authors do not suggest this would lead to permanent expression of the complete virus, but do note that if reverse transcription did occur in some people, it could have important effects. One such effect may be the positive effect of conferring enhanced immunity, but another could be the emergence of a serious adverse response by inducing a hyper-reactive immune system. This in turn could lead to complications such as a cytokine storm or an auto-immune reaction where the body turns on its own cells. A potential causal mechanism would be due to the immune system identifying those cells responsible for production of the antigen, which may itself be harmless, as problematic and attacking the whole cells. Additionally, endogenous production of antigens could lead to false-positives tests when using antigen-based tests such as the lateral flow test.

Both the Moderna and the Pfizer vaccines contain polyethylene glycol - PEG for short. PEG is commonly used in pharmaceuticals including medications, soaps, toothpaste, and processed food products. In the vaccine, it is used for stabilising and preserving the lipid nanoparticles used to wrap the mRNA. PEG had never been used in a vaccine before and it was identified early on as a potential cause of anaphylaxis in vaccine recipients although some experts seemed sceptical of this capability [339]. However, in 2016, a researcher identified PEG as a substance whose potency as an allergen may have been severely underestimated [340]. Evidence for such suspicions were supported by the finding that 72% of people tested had detectable antibodies to PEG. This indicates that their immune systems had been stimulated into action by some form of exposure to PEG and their bodies had identified PEG as an unwanted invader. 7% of those who develop such antibodies produce them at levels that may predispose them to anaphylaxis [341].

Polysorbate-80 is a surfactant. It is used in both the Johnson and Johnson, and the AstraZeneca vaccines. Surfactants are products that are designed to force two materials to mix that would otherwise separate, i.e., oil and water. The function and integrity of cell membranes is dependent on the maintenance of clearly defined hydrophilic and hydrophobic properties. As such, surfactants are not desirable things to have in the body. Polysorbate 80 has been used in many medical and food products such as ice cream, but few may be aware of its detrimental effects to the body. There is evidence that when ingested orally it can affect the mucosal barrier and permeability of the small intestine - increasing absorption of chemical pollutants, such as pesticides [342]. When present in the blood, polysorbate-80 has long been identified as a carrier substance that has potential to cause increased permeability of the blood brain barrier [343]. Its link as a vaccine ingredient that causes adverse reactions has previously been identified but a lack of awareness among the medical community about its biological impacts mean it is rarely linked to adverse reactions [344]. It has been found to cause inflammation, ulcers, and hyperplasia (enlarged organs) in animal experiments, and increase oxidative stress in cells contributing to cytotoxicity (poisoning of the cells) [345, 346].

One group of medical experts, writing in the journal 'Vaccine', suggest that there was clear need for more research into anaphylaxis linked to the new mRNA vaccine ingredients, specifically referring to the Pfizer and Moderna products [347]. They highlighted a number of ingredients with potential to cause allergic responses and noted:

The ionizable lipids that are used in both vaccines are novel amino-lipids and their allergenic potential is not known.

This proves that the administration of such ingredients into human beings was experimental. However, it was a poorly designed experiment. A disciplined scientific experiment to test these ingredients would need to trial them separately from other ingredients to control for conflating observed effects with those caused by other ingredients or through synergistic responses with them. Indeed, a thorough experiment would require each combination of ingredients to be tested individually to determine potential complications arising from a specific single ingredient or any combination of them. None of this was considered necessary by the vaccine manufacturers. The safety tests that were conducted for the Pfizer vaccine excluded single dose toxicity, toxicokinetics (how the body metabolises and excretes the substance), genotoxicity and carcinogenicity. Remember, we are not simply talking about the spike protein mRNA here, we are talking about a host of ingredients, some of which are novel, or being administered in a novel way. Further concerns, and more evidence of the experimental nature of the vaccines, were raised by authors of a paper published in the journal 'Toxicology Reports' in April 2021 [348]:

Data on long-term studies, interaction with other vaccines, use in pregnancy/breast-feeding, use in immunocompromised subjects, and in subjects with co-morbidities, autoimmune or inflammatory disorders are still missing for these vaccines.

Adding to concern about autoimmunity is evidence that the illness, COVID-19, is not simply about the direct effects of the virus but may be significantly associated with virus-induced autoimmune pathology. Research suggests that infection with SARS-CoV-2 can lead to an autoimmune response against phospholipids in cells of endothelial tissue; it is possible that vaccines could induce anti-phospholipid antibodies which would cause an immune response leading to immunothrombosis [349].

<u>vii. Vaccine-Induced Viral Evolution</u>

Just like living organisms, viruses evolve under selective pressure. This means that they are capable of mutating into versions that are not as susceptible to vaccine-induced immune response or that may be more capable of using the response to their advantage via ADE. In 2017, a paper was published that sought to examine the reason why vaccine resistance was relatively rare (not none-extant); it noted several examples where vaccine programs had appeared to lead to vaccine-resistant mutations [350]. The authors suggested that the vaccines most at risk of inducing vaccine resistant mutation are those that are effective in reducing disease but do not prevent infection, replication, and transmission. The explanation is simple. While the virus is replicating in the body, some replicants will be the result of random mutations. Those which produce serotypes (distinct variations) with antigens that are not targeted, or ineffectively targeted, by the vaccine-induced immune response will be more likely to survive. The survivors of this selective pressure then become highly capable of replication and transmission. Once transmission of the mutated virus occurs, the new host may be susceptible to infectious disease regardless of whether they have been vaccinated and hence a new round of transmission occurs. People with natural immunity are likely to have a more complex immune response including a greater diversity of antibodies targeting various parts of the virus. As such they will be more likely to resist the new infectious agent or if they do get infected, recover more quickly. This gives the virus less chance to replicate and less chance of a significant variant emerging. However, in vaccinated people, the antigen response is narrow and if a replicant emerges that evades this, it may lead to a prolonged infection, greater spread, and increased chance of further mutations occurring. The result could be the creation of a more dangerous pathogen than the one the vaccine was initially intended to protect against. The risk of this occurring is connected with the diversity of vaccine-induced immune response.

One of the few viral vaccines known to have induced rapid vaccine resistance was the hepatitis B virus (HPV). It is believed to be due to the vaccine lacking multiple antigenic targets. Multiple targets means that the immune response is directed at different parts of the virus. Hence, if a replicant is the product of mutation in a way that evades one specific immune response, other targets are likely to remain and the virus will still be neutralised. However, if there was only one target antigen in the vaccine and a mutation produced a replicant capable of evading immune detection, then vaccine-induced immunity would become ineffective.

The SARS-CoV-2 vaccines only target the spike protein. When they were launched, we were told that the vaccines would not *prevent* infection, would not *stop* replication, and would not *halt* transmission, they were only found to be successful at reducing the severity of the disease, reducing hospitalisation, and were expected to reduce transmission [352, 353]. All evidence in support of this was derived from short-term studies. Hence, there was a plausible mechanism for selective pressure to produce new vaccine resistant versions of the virus and no evidence to prove that this could not happen. A report released by UK government's SAGE committee in July 2021 confirmed the risk of the emergence of vaccine resistant variants stating [354, 355]:

> *...an increase in morbidity and mortality would be expected even in the face of vaccination since vaccines do not provide absolute sterilising immunity i.e. **they do not fully prevent infection in most people*** [emphasis added].

Within the same report, SAGE confirmed that there was a 'realistic' likelihood of the emergence of a significantly more virulent and deadly strain than had previously been seen. Additional discussion confirms how evolutionary processes may lead to the emergence of new variants of SARS-CoV-2 but shamefully the document is devoid of any mention of how vaccines might create the precise pressures that contribute to driving the emergence of more deadly strains than might occur without them. This is likely due to the cognitive bias and conflicts of interest of the authors (who were too coy to bother putting their names on the taxpayer-funded report).

Marek's disease is a classic example of a case where vaccines have driven the emergence of variants which are both vaccine-resistant and much more deadly to the unvaccinated than is likely to have occurred naturally. The disease, a serious nuisance for poultry farmers, was first identified early in the 20th century by Joszef Marek. Nonetheless, the poultry industry survived for a further half a century before a vaccine was introduced. However, once it was, the severity of the disease became much worse due to vaccine-induced viral evolution. Vaccinated chickens became more likely to shed more virulent variants than non-vaccinated chickens [356]. The new variants became more deadly to the non-vaccinated population and eventually led to a situation where all chickens had to be vaccinated or they would be certain to die. It is possible that the SARS-CoV-2 vaccine program could stimulate selective pressures leading to emergence of more virulent types. This is not a dissimilar process to how other diseases evade treatment, including the way superbugs emerge in response to the over-use of antibiotics. As SARS-CoV-2 was a newly identified virus and the experimental vaccines had not been subject to intense longitudinal studies, the likelihood of such a development was not known. However, corona viruses are known to be highly adaptive and capable of constant mutation. This is why those that cause the common cold have never been eradicated. Given the reported appearance of numerous new strains of SARS-CoV-2 during 2020 and 2021 it is clear that SARS-CoV-2 is capable of rapid evolution under selective pressure. However, it is probably only coincidence that early variants that the UK government labelled as variants of concern arose in countries which conducted some of the earliest large-cohort SARS-CoV-2 vaccine trials - Brazil, India, and the UK.

Professor Luc Montagnier, a Nobel prize winner, stated publicly that he believed vaccines were driving the evolution of variants, and even believed that spikes in cases and mortality that show high correlation with the onset of vaccination programs, and appearance of new variants, may indicate that this is the case [357]. His views were not popular.

Significant, and potentially vaccine-resistant, mutation is something which becomes more likely as immunity increases within the population, be it natural or vaccine-acquired [358]. It is plausible that the vaccination program could induce the spread of ever more virulent variants which could produce a far deadlier pandemic than was seen in 2020-2021. This is especially the case if combined with the potential effects of antibody-dependent enhancement and pathogenic priming. A similar view, although perhaps argued with more

100

vigour, was published in an open letter by Geert Vanden Bossche PhD in February 2021 [359]. Vanden Bossche is an expert virologist and was a former senior programme officer with the Bill and Melinda Gates foundation. In his letter, he suggested that the ongoing experimental mass vaccination programme is:

...likely to become the biggest and most tragic mistake made in the history of public health in general and in the field of vaccination in particular.

Research published in April 2021, provided laboratory confirmed evidence that vaccinated people were becoming sources of variants that were capable of escaping the immune response induced via vaccination [360]. Some of the variants detected had significant mutations in the spike protein suggesting that the virus was indeed evolving to escape the antibodies created by the vaccine-induced humoral immune response. The humoral response is one that leads to the production of antibodies. Importantly, the authors concluded that this was clear evidence that vaccines were poor at inducing cross-neutralisation against mutations in the receptor binding domain (part of the spike protein). Further research, published in July 2021, confirmed that the humoral response elicited from vaccination against the 'delta' variant was significantly less effective than against earlier versions of the virus [361]. The researchers also suggested that humoral response from patients who had recovered from earlier versions of the virus was also much less effective. Unfortunately, the research did not elicit any information on cellular immunity which the authors confessed may provide significant cross-reactive immunity when subject to real-life exposure. Without knowing this it is not credible to draw conclusions from this study about the efficacy of natural immunity in the face of variants. However, the study was a clear indication that vaccines may confer limited protection even in the short term as they do not invoke complex cross-reactive immunity. The implications for long-term vaccine-acquired immunity would be bleak.

A particularly worrisome possibility is the potential for continuing schemes of mass vaccination and 'top-up' vaccines to create a situation where the disease evolves to become so deadly that only the vaccinated survive. This is what happened with Marek's disease following decades in which chicks were subject to inoculation regimes as standard practice. Not only did the vaccination program create an evolutionary pressure, driving selection of more virulent strains, but natural selective pressure, that would ordinarily operate to promote adaptive natural resistance in the target population, was eliminated because of vaccination [356]. The fact that humans are not chickens does not invalidate comparison of the processes of adaptive evolution. It is not unimaginable for a continual program of vaccine boosters to fail suddenly and catastrophically, either due to mutation or due to a sudden failure in vaccine supply. The commentariat who suggested that it may be necessary to implement a regular program of annual or biannual vaccines for SARS-CoV-2, and its variants, do not appear to acknowledge or understand the severity of this risk, instead focusing on the short-term, as is habitual in modern times [362, 363].

The converse may also be true. Vaccines could drive the virus to evolve in such a way that only the unvaccinated survive. This could happen if a mutation conferred upon a virus the ability to make effective use of antibody-dependent enhancement (ADE) – in this instance, specifically with regard to utilising a spike protein antibody. To recap, ADE is where the virus makes use of an antibody to enter a macrophage where, instead of being destroyed, it can harness the immune cell in order to replicate. People who have been vaccinated, but not experienced a natural infection, may not have the sort of complex cross-reactivity that might arise from natural infection. Even people who have suffered a natural infection but have also been vaccinated may have an immune system skewed to favour production of spike protein antibodies. For these people, their antigen-specific immune defence will be entirely, or mostly, oriented toward making spike protein antibodies. A viral variant that becomes capable of using these antibodies to enter cells and replicate, will turn this defence mechanism into an enhanced means of attack. Such a variant would then be capable of replicating extremely quickly in people who have a high presence of spike protein antibodies, or whose immune memory cells cause them to quickly create them before other antibodies, targeting different antigens, are produced. Indeed, mass vaccination, which almost exclusively targets the spike protein, creates an evolutionary pressure for this to occur. It does not mean it will definitely happen, but the likelihood is increased, and the potential consequences are dire.

Another potential concern with the vaccines involves the outside chance of reverse transcription occurring. Retroviruses insert their RNA into human cell DNA using an enzyme - reverse transcriptase - but the process is prone to error and can easily result in the DNA encoding a mutated version of the virus. SARS-CoV-2 is not known to be a retrovirus, but there may be potential for the modified RNA contained in gene-based vaccines to be reverse transcribed into core cell DNA, either by the reverse transcriptase that is endogenous to human cells, or by viral reverse transcriptase in people infected with retroviruses. A person's body could then become capable of producing proteins similar to the spike protein, or parts of it, which may induce an autoimmune response. However, should this possibility materialise, patients would likely experience symptoms of chronic illness similar to those where immunopathology is implicated such as chronic fatigue and inflammatory disorders. These conditions may result in disability, suffering, and long-term demise but might never be associated with their true cause. Links between vaccination and immune pathology is not lacking evidence. For example, in 2017, a systematic review of published scientific evidence found a very strong correlation between vaccination and the immune disorders of Systemic Lupus Erythematosus and Rheumatoid Arthritis [351].

viii. <u>Unlisted Vaccine Ingredients</u>

Vaccine-induced injury may also be caused by ingredients that are not even supposed to be present and are not listed on the vaccine information sheet. For example, analysis of an HPV vaccine branded 'Gardasil' has shown it to contain both toluene and benzene-based compounds [364]. These are volatile organic compounds used in the manufacturing process to extract immunogenic peptides. They should be removed from the final product but are easily absorbed by silicone - an ingredient present in the vaccine concoction. When the volatile organic compounds are not thoroughly removed, they may get injected into the body along with the vaccine and cause dysfunction of voltage-gated sodium and calcium channels, a problem that can be exacerbated by synergistic effects caused by the silicone.

Disrupted voltage-gated ion (i.e., calcium – Ca2+ and sodium – Na+) channels are particularly problematic and can disrupt biochemical signalling pathways and cause severe dysfunction of the brain. The problem does not affect everybody but only those individuals that are susceptible. However, once triggered, these physical problems may become self-sustaining and develop into chronic disease. Due to the novel make-up, complex processing, high volume of manufacture, and number of different production facilities involved in the creation of COVID-19 vaccines and their ingredients, contamination will always be a risk. Indeed, regulators shut down a production facility in Baltimore when it found unlisted ingredients were mistakenly being added during the manufacture of the Johnson and Johnson vaccine [365].

ix. Prion Disease

The SARS-CoV-2 spike protein appears to be capable of passing into the brain and has qualities that show the potential to trigger neurodegenerative diseases associated with prion production and amyloid formation [366, 367]. Endogenous production of the spike protein is the primary action of most available COVID-19 vaccines. Research has also found that the spike protein alone has the capability of causing lung damage [368] and may be capable of altering gene expression in airway cells [369]. Another group of researchers have suggested that [370]:

...the SARS-CoV-2 spike protein (without the rest of the viral components) triggers cell signalling events that may promote pulmonary vascular remodelling and PAH [pulmonary arterial hypertension] as well as possibly other cardiovascular complications.

Indeed, the growing evidence of potential harm resulting from the spike protein alone led Dr Bryam Bridle, an associate professor who has been involved in mRNA vaccine research for decades, to say [371]:

The spike protein is a pathogenic protein, it is a toxin, it can cause damage in our body...we made a big mistake...we thought the spike protein was a great target antigen, we never knew the spike protein itself was a toxin.

Additional concern was raised by further research that found that adenovirus-based vaccines, intended to promote endogenous spike protein production, could lead to the creation of soluble spike protein variants which could be linked to problems with thromboses [306]. Those affected effectively suffer from a severe illness or even death that mimics the more severe effects of a wild virus infection but is in fact induced by the vaccine.

Analysis of vaccine RNA sequences has also indicated potential for the formation of pathogenic prions [372]. Prions and amyloids are proteins that, for some reason, become misshapen and are resistant to protease - enzymes that break down proteins. Proteins can be extremely complex in their structure but an often overlooked, yet essential, aspect of their function arises from the way in which they are folded. These shapes, which are often graphically represented in images that look like untidy balls of string, confer upon the protein special qualities related to the position of the atoms and patterns of electric charge. A protein that is normally functional and healthy to have in the body can become misshapen, or misfolded, sometimes leading it to become problematic. In prion disease, the prion has a catalytic mode of action and prionic proteins can proliferate, causing a cascading effect over time which can eventually lead to serious illness. An example of a prion-type disease is CJD (Creutzfeldt-Jakob Disease), also known as mad cow's disease. The brain is affected. Over time there is a loss of function and death. The early stages of the disease can be particularly distressing as the cause of neurological symptoms such as mood swings, memory loss, temporary nerve dysfunction, shaking, flashing lights etc. might be unknown and difficult to diagnose for some time. A case of CJD associated with onset of COVID-19 has already been recorded but may be coincidental [373]. Prion-type diseases can take years to decades to develop. Should they emerge, there would need to be expert analysis of statistical evidence from substantial cohorts of vaccinated and unvaccinated populations, potentially including factors such as infection with wild-virus, type of vaccine received and the number of inoculations administered, in order to be able to spot any causal links.

<u>x. Negligence and Errors in Handling and Administering Inoculation</u>

Most discussions around vaccine safety concerns are misleadingly simplistic. Not only do they omit some of the most important risks which have already been discussed, but they also ignore significant risks arising from poor practice on behalf of those handling and administering the vaccine. According to Public Health England these risks include: incorrect dosage, expired vaccine, inoculation at inappropriate intervals, inappropriate site, poor technique or route of administration, use of the wrong diluent, incorrect preparation, contamination, incorrect storage, and contraindications being ignored [374]. Numerous reports have confirmed these risks are real. In one case, a cleaner in Boston was reported as having accidentally disconnected the power supply to a freezer storing vaccines [375]. The facility in which this occurred was supposed to be restricted and should have been inaccessible to the cleaner. An alarm also failed to activate. Several other storage errors have been reported, one incident occurred when vials were removed from a freezer intentionally, another when people were vaccinated using product that had been stored at temperatures which were too low [376, 377, 378].

Numerous instances of recipients only receiving injections of saline have been reported in the US, Canada, and Japan, where over fifty people including medical professionals were accidentally injected with saline that had not been mixed with the active vaccine [379, 380, 381, 382]. There are also reports of mistakes in inoculations that took place in Hong Kong, Canada, and Australia, contravening patient choice and medical guidelines designed to protect vulnerable people [383, 384, 385]. Vaccine that had passed its use by date was injected into over 899 people at a pop-up site in New York [386]. In British Columbia, Canada, twelve children were accidentally vaccinated with a brand of vaccine that had not yet received emergency use authorisation for their age group [387]. A similar event in Australia saw 163 children 'accidentally' vaccinated with the Pfizer mRNA vaccine which was contrary to national policy at the time [388]. Regardless of whether there were any direct consequences, there were detailed and important protocols to be followed in storing, preparing, and administering vaccines - not even knowing which one is being administered is breath-taking negligence.

xi. Manufacturing Irregularities

Manufacturing mRNA vaccines is a particularly sensitive process and the potential for things to go awry is high, something that does not appear to have been discussed in popular media. However, the issue was raised following the revelation of leaked emails that had been acquired from the European Medical Agency (EMA) by hackers. The emails revealed that analysis of some batches of the Pfizer vaccine examined by the EMA were found to have anomalies in the contents, including significantly lower levels of vaccine-related mRNA and 'truncated and modified mRNA species present in the finished product' [389]. Not only could these manufacturing irregularities lead to ineffective doses, they also show how unstable mRNA is; the exact nature of the modified mRNA and what it might have coded for has not been disclosed.

Clearly, errors in manufacturing are a potential risk. Early in 2021, a disturbing report revealed that a plant manufacturing vaccines for J&J had contaminated millions of doses with the wrong ingredients. The problem was not discovered or disclosed by the manufacturer and was only brought to light following an inspection carried out by a government agency [390]. Further concerns were raised by researchers who found AstraZeneca vaccine contaminated with human protein and other unwanted unstructural proteins; analysis confirmed the presence of over one thousand human-protein derived peptides suggested to originate from the human cell line (cultured from kidney cell lines that originate from an aborted human foetus) used in the culture of the adenovirus vector [391]. These peptides are not supposed to be present in the finished product and many 'fact-checkers' claim that they are not present in the vaccine. They may wish to recheck their 'facts'. The researchers suggested that ELISA tests used to check for unwanted ingredients may be ineffective and implementing thorough and effective quality control could be extremely time-consuming. They also state that some of the unwanted contaminants were present in large enough amounts to have the potential to cause short-term adverse reactions and long-term autoimmune pathologies.

xii. Terrorism, Sabotage, and Fraud

Additional threats come from the use of fake vaccines - thousands of which were found circulating in China and South Africa [392]. In India, thousands were injected with sea water by a group, including a doctor, who were perpetrating deliberate fraud [393]. Sabotage is also a potential concern, heightened by the threat of hacking. Already, one hacking attack is known to have occurred and believed to have originated from a state actor attempting to target and interfere with systems controlling cold storage [394]. Interest in intercepting or interfering with vaccine supply could arise from nation states or terrorist groups. Other concerns over hacking relate to sophisticated attacks that interfere with the data used to sequence DNA, mRNA, or control recipes, including excipient concentration levels [395]. An attack of this sort could lead to widespread inoculation with DNA or RNA that expressed biotoxins, caused prion-type diseases, created long-term chronic health problems, or induced cancer.

The effects of such an attack might not be immediately obvious and may only be uncovered if vaccine batches and recipients were being monitored and compared with control groups over a substantial period of time. Given the uncountable number of competing nations and factions, including the rise in threats of military conflict between major powers, and the never-ending accounts of poor design, mistakes, and vulnerabilities within IT systems, the use of stealth sabotage must be taken seriously.

xiii. Conclusion

There are diverse, serious, and substantial short and long-term risks associated with COVID-19 vaccines. Their medium and long-term efficacy is not known. Some of the potential harmful effects of a mass vaccination program could be significantly more catastrophic than the original pandemic. We must hope that they do not come to fruition. As of the 21st of July 2021, over 1 million post-vaccine adverse reactions, affecting over 330 thousand people, had been reported and recorded on the MHRA yellow card scheme for the three vaccines in use in the UK (Pfizer, AstraZeneca, and Moderna). These reactions included, but are not limited to [396]:

- 1,257 cases of anaphylaxis
- 411 cases of thrombo-embolic events with concurrent low platelets of which:
- 146 cases were cerebral venous thrombosis
- 265 cases were major thromboembolic events with thrombocytopenia
- 73 out of the 411 died, 30 were people under 50 years old
- 9 cases of capillary leak syndrome
- 27, 510 cases of menstrual disorders
- 16,593 blood disorders
- 13,184 heart disorders
- 4,493 immune disorders
- 362 cases of Guillain-Barre syndrome
- 13,312 cases of ear disorders
- 18,130 eye disorders
- 1,517 deaths were reported as potentially linked to vaccination

The MHRA explained all of this away by saying they have compared incidence rates to background data and found nothing unusual. They also suggested that there will be more reports than are valid because of the black triangle status of the vaccines which requires all suspected side effects to be reported regardless of whether there was any evidence for a causal connection. However, they provided no evidence-based analysis for their assertion nor any report that is open to public or academic scrutiny. In effect they made nothing more than an assumption followed by an authoritarian diktat. As has already been shown, the weight of evidence suggests that there is far more likely to be massive under-reporting of side effects not over reporting. So, based on that evidence, not the assumptions of an organisation rife with conflicts of interest and who are directly responsible for pushing the vaccine on the UK public, the above figures are likely to be around 5-15% of the actual occurrences. It must also be noted that while some of the reported side effects may seem remote from a vaccine, and some will no doubt not be related, others may be connected with as yet unidentified causal mechanisms.

The potential for the vaccines to cause minor clots in blood vessels anywhere in the body could cause a wide variety of varying symptoms such as localised discomfort, partial organ damage, pain, pins and needles, and so on. Small blockages could lead to greater damage over time. Issues such as myocarditis that appears to resolve could leave a permanently damaged heart that one day leads to death. Other symptoms or disorders that have a slow onset and produce chronic problems that gradually worsen and/or become chronic over time, such as autoimmune disorders, neurological problems, heart disease, cancer, gradual loss of sight etc., are unlikely to ever be associated with the vaccine and hence will not be reported or investigated. Remember the debate about HPV vaccine and its association with cancer is still ongoing after decades and asbestos was in use for well over a century before its carcinogenic properties were even suspected. And we should never forget that doctors once helped promote cigarette smoking, and called thalidomide harmless. Experts can be misguided and are capable of making serious errors of fact, and errors of judgement.

Perhaps if those pushing vaccines for the last half-century had been obliged to be more realistic about their claims and were held accountable for their products, both criminally and financially, the industry would have been forced to evolve. Perhaps science would have been forced to grapple with the complexity and marvel of human biology and would have developed a much more thorough understanding of the dynamic interaction of the body, the immune system, and the environment. Maybe there would be more awareness of the potential long-term disbenefits, or costly ineffectiveness, of mass vaccination programs. Perhaps we would by now have a different, and more effective, understanding of how to manage infectious disease.

Sadly, honesty and integrity are rare commodities in a world driven by short-term thinking and self-interest. It may be time to re-evaluate the liability-free status of the vaccine industry and to tackle the corporate-political entrenchment of their privileged status. It is unlikely this will happen. Drugs are big money, and vaccine manufacturers and its associated lobby are highly influential. Their income and power continue to grow. In 2000, the vaccine market was estimated to be worth $5 billion, by 2017 this had grown to $34 billion and forecasts suggest that by 2026 the vaccine market will be worth $81.5 billion [397, 398]. One wonders if this predicted meteoric rise would have been tempered if other effective treatments and prophylactic treatments had been recommended for use early on. At least nine industry leaders have become billionaires as the result of profits and rising stock prices associated with COVID-19 vaccine development [399].

Considering the levels of coercion, blinkered thinking, and relentless propaganda, it is pertinent to ask whether the full risks of SARS-CoV-2 vaccines, and uncertainties over the benefits, have really been disclosed to vaccine recipients so as to meet medical ethics standards on informed consent. Equally important, is to ask whether the public at large were fully informed about the fact that most people who catch the disease had minor symptoms and recovered quickly without treatment, and that those people will likely have developed long-lasting natural immunity that protects them and those around them; a more robust protection than vaccines are likely to provide. Additionally, many treatments exist with substantive evidence of improving recovery rates significantly without the need for taking any chances with the known and unknown risk of the novel vaccines if they are deployed soon enough after an infection has been identified.

6. Treatment

For those few who were more at risk from COVID-19, many treatment options were available; some of these were known to be effective very early after the emergence of the SARS-CoV-2 virus. As such, the use of an experimental vaccine that has had no long-term safety studies for disease control is a risky business and really should have been considered as a last option, not the first, in combatting a newly emerging disease. Where effective treatments and prophylactics are available, experimenting with novel vaccine technology on unwitting and poorly informed human populations should not be deemed necessary and never mandatory. A prophylactic is something that is used before contracting an infection or disease whereas a treatment is something used afterwards. Treatments and prophylactics share similar goals: to reduce severity, encourage recovery, and enable the development of natural immunity. Unlike a treatment, a fully effective prophylactic can also serve to prevent infection or disease arising following exposure to a pathogen. The following treatments are cheap and freely available, they have had decades of long-term usage so that short-term, medium-term, and long-term risks are well known. However, their widespread use and deployment was unlikely to have had the sort of dramatic effects on stocks and shares as the novel COVID-19 vaccines did.

a. Chloroquine and Hydroxychloroquine

Chloroquine was first identified as an effective prophylactic and treatment for corona virus in 2005 following trials conducted on mice that had been deliberately infected with the SARS-CoV virus [400]. Hydroxychloroquine is very similar to chloroquine but considered less toxic. Both drugs have been used for decades to prevent malaria and treat chronic inflammation arising from auto-immune diseases such as lupus and rheumatoid arthritis. In many countries they are considered so safe that they are freely available to buy over the counter and without prescription.

A large cohort of qualified and practising doctors in America were so confident of its efficacy, and yet so concerned about authorities trying to prevent its use, that they formed a group called America's Frontline Doctors in order to inform the public of their opinion. During the summer of 2020 they produced a video in which they explained their position and their clinical experience of using the drug successfully in the treatment of patients diagnosed with SARS-CoV-2. However, the video was censored from popular social media platforms and ignored by many media outlets. One of the reasons for this was due to a hastily published paper that appeared in the Lancet, a respected, peer-reviewed, scientific journal. The paper suggested hydroxychloroquine was ineffective and dangerous. This led the WHO to put a moratorium on the drug. However, after independent scrutiny and requests for the original data, which the authors refused to provide, the paper was later retracted [401]. It appeared that the data used in the study had been completely fabricated. Yes, a paper based on invented data, and designed to push a political narrative, was published in a major international journal following peer-review. This did not prevent individuals from America's Frontline Doctors from being persecuted. One committed and hard-working doctor was sacked from two hospitals [402]. Others were threatened, as were the staff they had worked with.

One of the key contentions in the hydroxychloroquine debate was over the fact that those who claimed to have used it effectively suggested it needed to be used sparingly early after infection and symptom onset, whereas the data relied upon for evidence against it was focused on post-hospitalised patients receiving absurdly large, and toxic, doses. There is often an absence of the sort of data academics rely upon for analysis when a treatment is first used in a novel way or on a novel disease. This would not ordinarily prevent its use and important factors such as direct clinical experience and expertise, alongside patient choice would come to the fore. New York Doctor, Vladimir Zelenko, claimed to have treated over 1000 patients using a low dose of hydroxychloroquine alongside zinc and an antibiotic, with only three high-risk individuals having succumbed to death by COVID-19, the rest recovering [403].

A thorough review and explanation of the mechanisms of Hydroxychloroquine suggest that there is good evidence to show that it can be an effective treatment when used as part of a combinational therapy regime, but there is also evidence that questions its efficacy and there are dangers in its use at higher doses [404]. When contemplated as a single body of data, without paying attention to the nuance in the way the drug is deployed, the evidence appears conflicting and uncertain. In the USA, the FDA stopped the use of Chloroquine and Hydroxychloroquine in summer of 2020 for treating COVID-19 (it is still available for other conditions). China chose to continue to permit the use of Chloroquine but not Hydroxychloroquine. A balanced analysis suggested that there was evidence of a significant effect in combatting the virus in some patients, especially when deployed early and with low doses [405]. It appeared that other methods and factors involved in its use were significant.

b. Vitamin D

The UK public body, the National Institute of Health and Care Excellence (NICE), suggest that, in the winter months between December and March, 39% of adults aged 19-64, and 32% of the under 19s, have low vitamin D [406]. In the summer (July to September) it is 8%

114

and 4% respectively – far fewer but still a significant number of people. NICE also state that people from minority ethnic groups, and those who live in institutions such as prisons and residential homes, may be more likely to have low vitamin D levels. The main reason for this is lack of sunlight. In the UK, sunlight is insufficient for skin to create vitamin D during the winter months and this loss cannot be accounted for through diet. People with darker skin are less able to make vitamin D naturally given equal exposure to sunlight and are more prone to vitamin D deficiency in geographical regions and/or seasons that have less sunlight. In 2020, Dr Fauci - the head of the US CDC - confirmed that vitamin D supplements can help strengthen the immune system to fight infection and confirmed that he took them himself [407].

Lower levels of vitamin D have been shown to be associated with higher disease severity and higher mortality rates among COVID-19 patients [407]. A systematic review and meta-analysis published in March 2021 concluded that those deficient in vitamin D were 80% more likely to develop a COVID-19 infection compared with those who were not deficient [409]. Almost half of children treated for COVID-19 infections were found to be vitamin D deficient [410]. Additional meta-analyses also showed a strong link between vitamin D supplementation and reduced chance of admission to intensive care along with reduced need for ventilation when treatment was required [411, 412]. The experts reviewing this evidence suggested that there were three significant causal explanations for the efficacy of vitamin D in assisting the body to resist COVID-19 infection. The first is by strengthening cellular immunity by inducing the production of antimicrobial peptides. The second is by stimulating genes related to the control of the integrity of cellular junctions helping to reduce inter-cellular invasion by microorganisms and reducing associated inflammation. Finally, most immune cells have a vitamin D receptor and presence of sufficient vitamin D can assist in modulating the immune response and preventing harmful hyper-immune reactions such as the cytokine storm which is associated with much of the serious complications of COVID-19. Obesity is associated with lower levels of vitamin D circulating in the body [413]. This is suspected to be due to it becoming locked up in excess fat tissue in the body which blocks its bioavailability [414]. It is known that COVID-19 patients who are obese suffer from worse symptoms and have significantly more negative outcomes, including death, than patients who are not obese [415].

c. Zinc

Globally, around 6% of mortality is attributable to inadequate intake of micronutrients - in 2019 that would have been just less than 2.5 million deaths; annually, around 1 billion are at risk from zinc deficiency due to inadequate dietary supply [416, 417]. Use of zinc sulphate in COVID-19 patients has been found to decrease both the severity and lethality of the disease [418]. When zinc has been used in combination with low doses of hydroxychloroquine and azithromycin (commonly used against pneumonia) it has been shown to reduce hospitalisation [419]. Lower blood levels of zinc were found to be associated with worse severity of disease and more negative outcomes for COVID-19 inpatients; lower levels of zinc also appeared to be associated with higher inflammatory response and consequent complications [420]. Research from 2010 had already shown that zinc helps to block corona virus from replicating in cells [421].

d. Ivermectin

A meta-analysis of 18 randomised controlled trials performed by a team led by Dr Pierre Kory show that Ivermectin is a highly effective drug in reducing mortality, decreasing the length of recovery time from COVID-19 infection, and, when deployed as a preventative medicine, in significantly reducing the risk of contracting infection [422]. Kory and his team found that when deployed across large populations as a prophylactic, the effects on reducing incidence of disease have been dramatically positive. Ivermectin has been used in human medicine since the 1980s and is classed as an essential medicine by the WHO as it can be used against parasites and viruses and is extremely safe. Its efficacy against COVID-19 is suspected to be related to its anti-inflammatory properties and capacity for reducing complications associated with the cytokine storm. When used as a prophylactic it has been reported to reduce viral transmission five-fold. It has potential to be more effective

116

and less risk-laden than COVID-19 vaccines and comes with decades of long-term safety data (as opposed to none for the novel vaccines). However, as of August 2021, key medical agencies such as the WHO, the US CDC, and European Medicines Agency, continued to suggest evidence for use of Ivermectin is uncertain and, despite being gung-ho for experimental mRNA vaccines, that use entirely novel methods and ingredients and have no long-term safety or efficacy data, they had not approved Ivermectin even for emergency use.

Ivermectin is produced as a generic drug by multiple manufacturers, it is not a huge profit maker. The refusal of agencies to base their decisions on full consideration of the evidence is, at the very least, a little suspicious. Especially so, given that, along with a host of colleagues, Dr Tess Laurie has provided ample evidence of the efficacy of ivermectin via a systematic review, meta-analysis, and trial sequential analysis, that included 24 randomised controlled trials; this evidence showed that infection rates could be reduced by up to 86% [423]. Use of ivermectin has been found to reduce mortality from COVID-19 infection by around 56% [424]. Dr Laurie is a consultant who has made a living working with teams of experts to thoroughly review medicines for approval for organisations including the NHS. Her work is of the highest standard in forensically examining evidence for the use of medicines. Not only has her evidence been ignored but, like many other highly qualified and highly intelligent people who have failed to acquiesce to expected narratives, she had been actively attacked and censored. One detailed and damning review by expert scientific journalist Edmund Fordham considers the failure to deploy Ivermectin a scandal and suggests that [425]:

At some point, officials who obstruct access to safe medicines are going to have to explain the moral difference between their actions and corporate manslaughter.

In the USA, a consortium of doctors and health professionals who had worked on the front line of health care during 2020, formed an organisation called Front Line COVID-19 Critical Care Alliance (FLCCC). Ivermectin was one of the drugs they recommended. They produced protocols called I-MASS, MATH+, I-MASK+ and I-RECOVER to help inform other health professionals on methods for preventing COVID-19 infection, for home and hospital treatment, and for use in recovery from long-term debilitating effects of the illness [426]. These protocols involved the use of cheap, commonly available vitamins and drugs that had been in use for a long time and had plenty of evidence of long-term safety from use in other applications for which they had FDA approval. The protocols were made available freely along with supporting evidence. They were ignored by the establishment.

7. Facemasks

Given that the wearing of a face mask became mandated for at least some settings in most countries, it could be expected that this policy would have been formed on the basis of solid scientific evidence. When people who refused to wear masks were subject to public derision, violence, police brutality, arrest and punishment, any reasonable person would assume that it must have been necessary for policy makers to show robust evidence that the wearing of masks actually worked in disease control and had no undesirable physical or psychological effects. However, there was no good evidence that the wearing of facemasks would be beneficial and plenty of evidence that they could cause harm. Not just short-term minor harm but potentially chronic and fatal disease.

a. Benefits

Prior to the COVID-19 outbreak, it was well known that facemasks were of little use for controlling or containing respiratory viruses. Early in 2020, Dr Fauci, a man who had worked on disease control for over forty years, including work with severe respiratory viruses, stated his position clearly [427]:

Indeed, examining the evidence suggests that his initial position, rather than his later U-turn, was the most scientifically credible one. A meta-analysis of ten randomised controlled trials that looked at the efficacy of non-pharmaceutical measures in controlling the spread of influenza found that the wearing of masks does not reduce viral transmission - the study was published on the CDC website in May 2020 [428]. In fact, it has long been known that facemasks have dubious efficacy even in a hospital setting. One study published in 1981, found that not wearing masks for six months during surgery showed no increase incidence of wound infection compared with wearing masks [429]. Cloth masks including homemade and improvised masks were often recommended by authorities and popular media. Indeed, a whole industry arose selling this type of mask. Yet evidence pre-dating COVID-19 found that cloth masks are almost entirely useless at stopping any particles from passing through, but are warm and can retain moisture acting as a reservoir and breeding ground for pathogens [432].

The use of facemasks by dentists to prevent the spread of airborne pathogens, was subject of a thorough review published in October 2016 [430]. It concluded that there was no evidence that the masks worked to prevent transmission. Among the many studies and reasons provided was the fact that masks were incapable of filtering 85% of particles sized between 0.3 and 2 microns - viral particles are far smaller, generally 0.04 - 0.1 microns - all of them can pass through either disposable medical-style facemasks or cloth masks. The tiny number that are blocked in the first instance will simply be dislodged and blown out via the sides or through the material on a subsequent inhalation and exhalation cycle. The author of the study called the policy of wearing facemasks as PPE nothing more than a fable.

A large randomised controlled study carried out in Denmark found no statistically significant difference between mask wearers and non-mask wearers in risk of testing positive for SARS-CoV-2 [431]. The authors of the paper appeared to go to great lengths to suggest that their study should not be used to question the efficacy of mask wearing despite their evidence being quite clear that masks were ineffective; bizarrely they attempted to suggest that their evidence could be used to argue that facemasks might be effective despite the range of uncertainty in their statistical analysis also showing that they could potentially increase infection. In terms of the statistical power of the samples used in the analysis, the study is probably best ignored. However, one of the reasons that the study was scientifically inconclusive was because so few people actually contracted the virus in either the mask wearing group or the non-mask wearing group out of the thousands recruited to take part - that is the most interesting fact revealed. This low infection rate occurred despite the participants being active in Denmark, a country where few people among the general population were wearing masks at the time the study was conducted. In the USA, a cross-state study in the USA found that mask wearing was not associated with increased containment of COVID-19 [438].

Perhaps the most damning assessment of the lack of efficacy of facemasks, came from Denis G. Rancourt PhD in April 2020 [433]. Rancourt had searched for randomised controlled trials that provided evidence that masks could be efficacious in the control of respiratory viruses. He found none, but did find numerous studies that show that masks are useless in the control of respiratory viruses [434, 435, 436, 437]. Having considered over 20 scientific papers relating to the issue he illustrated how studies that show control of droplets or larger particles are irrelevant when faced with the fact that aerosolised virions will always escape masks and be capable of causing infection. In other words, if someone is infectious, wearing a mask will not stop the virus escaping into the air. His conclusion was:

No RCT study with verified outcome shows a benefit for HCW [health care workers] or community members in households to wearing a mask or respirator. There is no such study. There are no exceptions. Likewise, no study exists that shows a benefit from a broad policy to wear masks in public.

He went on to say:

The present paper about masks illustrates the degree to which governments, the mainstream media, and institutional propagandists can decide to operate in a science vacuum, or select only incomplete science that serves their interests.

b. Harms

It would seem fairly obvious that putting something over your mouth and nose would affect your ability to breath. However, for those in doubt, there is science to support this. One study found that just six minutes of walking with a surgical mask on increases dyspnoea (shortness of breath) when compared with not wearing a mask [439]. Another research paper suggests that wearing a mask can lead to lowered levels of oxygen and increased levels of carbon dioxide (hypercapnic hypoxia) which [440]:

...may potentially increase acidic environment, cardiac overload, anaerobic metabolism and renal overload, which may substantially aggravate the underlying pathology of established chronic diseases.

For people wearing masks while exercising, significant reductions in blood oxygen, exercise performance, and an increase in shortness of breath were found [441]. The reduction of available oxygen was not found to have decreased to levels of clinical concern but it was physiologically measurable. A major shortcoming of the study, as with many others, is that it only looks at short-term use. Most studies use time periods of minutes. No studies appear to have been conducted examining the physiological effects of wearing facemask barriers for extended periods of time - such as the twelve hour plus shifts, day after day, as per health care workers who might be required to wear them.

Potential risk in pregnancy was raised as a potential safety concern by a study that showed prolonged use of an N95 mask under light physical activities could result in reduced oxygen intake and increased carbon dioxide retention [442]. The issue of oxygen deprivation was raised by another cohort of researchers who highlighted that mask wearing was associated with MIES - Mask Induced Exhaustion Syndrome [443]. The cohort provided

122

44 research papers showing a variety of issues arising due to the wearing of fabric, surgical, and N95 masks including: increased breathing resistance, increased respiratory rate, increased blood pressure, increased heart rate, respiratory impairment, fatigue, drowsiness, dizziness, headache, skin irritation, rhinitis, bacterial contamination, viral contamination, and fungal contamination. The study also listed research findings on detrimental psychological effects of mask wearing including a *false* sense of security and lowering of empathy. Psycho-vegetative effect was also evidenced - this is a condition that affects the mind and body usually connected with a psycho-somatic effect that influences endocrine and nervous system functioning creating real problems with the functioning of organs and unpleasant and distressing experiential symptoms.

Bacterial contamination is a serious issue as this can potentially lead to disease and death from sepsis and pneumonia. It is interesting to note that a study published in 2008 and co-authored by Dr Fauci of the CDC, concluded that the majority of deaths attributed to the Spanish flu pandemic of 1918 were most likely caused by secondary bacterial pneumonia [444]. Wearing improvised cloth facemasks was common during this period.

The risk of fungal contamination was linked to the outbreak of black fungus in India which was reported to have caused a large number of deaths during the pandemic. It was speculated that prolonged mask wearing accompanied by conditions of poor hygiene including low capacity for thorough and frequent washing of masks were contributory factors [445]. Addressing the issue of viral contamination, another group of researchers, whose work was published in 2019, examined masks worn by healthcare workers and found that prolonged mask-use could lead to general viral contamination of the outer surfaces increasing susceptibility for self-contamination and for carrying and retransmitting the viral load to others [446].

Disposable medical-style facemasks have been found to contain contaminant particulates including lead, cadmium, and antimony all of which can be directly harmful to human health including as respiratory irritants and carcinogens (i.e., antimony trioxide); they are also environmental pollutants [447]. Importantly, the type commonly acquired by the public, used by many businesses, and in care settings, are not manufactured to the standard of properly approved medical masks. As such, neither they, nor cloth masks, are permitted to be legally classified as personal protective equipment (PPE) or as a medical device [448, 449]. Concerned experts have found that there may be risk from the shedding and inhalation of micro-plastic particulates from masks [450]. Inhalation of microplastics could hold potential for causing chronic long-term respiratory problems as well as irritating and inflaming the respiratory tract which could make a person more prone to viral infection and complications associated with the immune response to such an infection. Such risks are contrary to legal requirements for the manufacture of safe products which stipulate that face coverings must [451]:

...be made from a fabric that does not shed fibres that may be inhaled during use.

These legal requirements also state:

Face covering not to be made from a material not designed to be worn against the skin or dyed with chemicals containing poisons that could be ingested.

c. Plastic Visors

Plastic visors are effectively useless as confirmed by SAGE in the UK [448]:

There is no published evidence that they are effective as a source control...

Guidance published by the UK government on the wearing of facemasks stated that [451]:

...face visors or shields do not adequately cover the nose and mouth, and do not filter airborne particles.

And,

...the government does not recommend their use by the wider public...

d. Summary

In March of 2020, the UK's chief medical officer, Chris Witty, stated that the public should not wear facemasks because they were of no use in controlling the spread of corona virus [452]. Despite poor evidence of efficacy, and plenty proving the potential harms caused by facemask wearing, many nations, including the UK, forced their citizens to wear them on fear of denial of entry to essential services such as supermarkets and hospitals. Despite clear exemptions being made, people without masks were frequently abused or assaulted by zealous members of the public, security guards, or police.

One case in Australia saw a man with heart disease suffer a heart attack following his arrest for not wearing a mask; militant police had refused to believe him when he told them he was not wearing a mask due to having a heart condition [453]. In spring of 2021, a case brought on behalf of a German school pupil resulted in the judge declaring that policies forcing children to wear facemasks were unconstitutional and causing physical, psychological, and pedagogical harm [454]. In July of 2021, the Telegraph reported the concerns of Dr Colin Axon, an advisor to the UK government. He compared facemasks to comfort blankets, noting that they do little to stop the spread of the virus which is approximately 500 000 times smaller than the pore size of most cloth masks [455]. Yet facemasks have become far more than comfort blankets. They are now closer to a pseudo-religious adornment and a symbol of the faithful to an irrational and godless religion.

8. Final Word

COVID-19 has brought about a world that is very different to the one that preceded it. Governments across the globe have mandated laws and controls over people that are contrary to the very idea of the sanctity and dignity of individual freedom. This has been done based on a pandemic that was declared on the grounds of a flawed testing system that abandoned the methods of rigorous science and standards applied to testing programs previously used for highly infectious disease. The application of this testing system also appears to have been adjusted so as to enable the most alarming narrative of crisis during 2020 and later, in 2021, altered in an attempt to paint a positive image of the effect of vaccination. Most cases for respiratory diseases peak in winter and drop in summer. This happened for COVID-19 in 2020 when there were no vaccines; when it happened in 2021 vaccines were heralded as the reason for the drop. Overall, deaths from COVID-19 appear to have been significantly over-reported and policies put in place that have undoubtedly led to tens of thousands of unnecessary deaths many of which may have been falsely attributed to the virus. Policies were implemented that led to economic, physiological, and psychological damage with detrimental effects on quality of life, morbidity, and mortality that will continue to have a significant impact for many years. The popular media have proven themselves incapable of real journalism or critical scientific reporting, instead choosing to obey and support government diktats helping to form a mass psychosis which shows no sign of ending; it is a mass psychosis that resembles those preceding historical atrocities.

Large swathes of the public are accepting entirely novel vaccines that are already associated with higher adverse events and deaths than all previous vaccines combined. They are being coaxed into swallowing the narrative that they are safe and effective despite plenty of evidence to the contrary and a complete absence of medium and long-term data on either safety or efficacy. Those who show concern about these new vaccines are labelled 'anti-vaxxers' even though most are merely trying to assert a preference about what is inserted into their own bodies. A decision which is irreversible. Most are not trying to dissuade or prevent others from getting a vaccine if they wish and many have no issue with traditional vaccines at all. The trope 'anti-vax' is a childish and disingenuous creation of the childish and disingenuous popular media. Smart people should avoid using it.

One of the most shocking outcomes of the pandemic is that it has led people to willingly subject themselves to being tracked and monitored electronically and to freely permit the government to restrict their movement, activity, and freedom of association with others. Freedoms that, in the past, millions have died to uphold and protect. People who are not infectious are being imprisoned in their homes or locked up against their will in quarantine centres, not on demonstrable or irrefutable evidence of infectivity, but on the premise that there is a small chance that they *might* be carrying a virus. A virus which as of August 2021, has a low fatality rate and from which most people either do not get sick or only have mild symptoms, recovering fully without any treatment, and going on to develop robust and broad immunity. Yes, many have died and, as with deaths from any cause, this is a sad and tragic loss. However, we all must face the eventuality that both we and our loved ones will, at some point, die from something. The question is whether the life we had before our demise was joyful, fulfilling, and worthwhile or whether it was fearful, timid, and servile.

Those suffering from government sponsored mass psychosis are already being positioned to support totalitarian forced-vaccination policies and centralised electronic vaccine passports. If implemented, they are likely to morph into a combination of an electronic global identification system combined with a geo-located electronic tagging system that can monitor movements, associations, activities, and biometrics with capabilities vastly beyond the coarse applications deployed in 2020 and 2021. Dissidents are being defamed, censored, and persecuted regardless of the veracity of their arguments which are dismissed, maligned, and smeared rather than engaged with in honest and open debate. Protest is being violently suppressed and mostly unreported, or is deliberately mischaracterised when it is. All the warnings and lessons from history appear to have been forgotten…again. When the amnesia wears off it may be too late.

Bibliography

1. Ortiz-Ospina, E. and Roser, M. (2016) *Trust*. Available at: https://ourworldindata.org/trust (Accessed: 18 07 2020)

2. Statista (2020) *Share of adults who trust news media most of the time in selected countries worldwide as of February 2020*. Available at: https://www.statista.com/statistics/308468/importance-brand-journalist-creating-trust-news/ (Accessed: 05 04 2021)

3. Textor, C. (2020) *Number of outbound tourists departing from China from 2010 to 2019*. Available at: https://www.statista.com/statistics/1068495/china-number-of-outbound-tourist-number/ (Accessed: 05 02 2021)

4. Menachery, V.D., Yount, B.L., Debbink, K., Agnihothram, S., Gralinski, L.E., Plante, J.A., Graham, R.L., Scobey, T., Ge, X.Y., Donaldson, E.F. and Randell, S.H. (2015) 'A SARS-like cluster of circulating bat coronaviruses shows potential for human emergence', *Nature Medicine*, *21*(12), pp.1508-1513.

5. Cyranoski, D. (2017) 'Inside the Chinese lab poised to study world's most dangerous pathogens', *Nature News*, *542*(7642), pp.399-401.

6. Rogin, J. (2021) Chaos Under Heaven: Trump, Xi, and the Battle for the Twenty-First Century. Boston: Houghton Mifflin Harcourt

7. Sparks, H. (2020) *No, coronavirus wasn't created by bio-terrorists in a lab*. Available at: https://nypost.com/2020/03/18/no-coronavirus-wasnt-created-by-bio-terrorists-in-a-lab/ (Accessed: 28 03 2020)

8. Daszak, P. (2020) *Ignore the conspiracy theories: scientists know Covid-19 wasn't created in a lab*. Available at: https://www.theguardian.com/commentisfree/2020/jun/09/conspiracies-covid-19-lab-false-pandemic/ (Accessed: 02 02 2021)

9. Husseini, S. (2020) *Peter Daszak's EcoHealth Alliance Has Hidden Almost $40 Million In Pentagon Funding And Militarized Pandemic Science*. Available at: https://www.independentsciencenews.org/news/peter-daszaks-ecohealth-alliance-has-hidden-almost-40-million-in-pentagon-funding/ (Accessed: 05 06 2021)

10. DeMarche, E. (2021) *Daszak 'recused' from Lancet's COVID-19 commission.* Available at: https://www.foxnews.com/health/daszak-recused-from-lancets-covid-19-commission (Accessed: 23 06 2021)

11. Abbasi, K. (2020) 'Covid-19: politicisation, "corruption," and suppression of science', *British Medical Journal*, 371(m4425)

12. RT News (2021) *Facebook says it will stop banning claims Covid-19 is man-made, citing 'new facts and trends'.* Available at: https://www.rt.com/usa/524915-facebook-covid-manmade-censorship/ (Accessed: 27 05 2021)

13. Pradhan, P., Pandey, A.K., Mishra, A., Gupta, P., Tripathi, P.K., Menon, M.B., Gomes, J., Vivekanandan, P. and Kundu, B. (2020) 'Uncanny similarity of unique inserts in the 2019-nCoV spike protein to HIV-1 gp120 and Gag', BioRxiv (Preprint)

14. Perawongmetha,A(2020) Unexpected side effect? Australia scraps Covid-19 vaccine development after trials lead to false positives for HIV. Available at: https://www.rt.com/news/509312-australia-coronavirus-vaccine-hiv-test/ (Accessed: 14 04 2021)

15. Andersen, K.G., Rambaut, A., Lipkin, W.I., Holmes, E.C. and Garry, R.F. 2020. The proximal origin of SARS-CoV-2. *Nature medicine*, 26(4), pp.450-452.

16. Winter, L (2020) *Chinese Officials Blame US Army for Coronavirus.* Available at: https://www.the-scientist.com/news-opinion/chinese-officials-blame-us-army-for-coronavirus-67267/ (Accessed: 20 04 2020)

17. Metro News (2020) *Theory coronavirus leaked from Chinese lab 'no longer discounted'.* Available at: https://metro.co.uk/2020/04/05/ministers-fear-coronavirus-might-leaked-lab-12510711/ (Accessed: 27 04 2020)

18. Awasthi, P. (2020) *French Nobel prize winner claims coronavirus came from Wuhan's lab.* Available at: https://www.thehindubusinessline.com/news/world/french-nobel-prize-winner-claims-coronavirus-came-from-wuhans-lab/article31385834 (Accessed: 20 04 2020)

19. RT News (2020) *Coronavirus was released from Chinese lab by 'accident', former MI6 chief claims, cites new study as proof.* Available at: https://www.rt.com/news/490714-mi6-china-lab-coronavirus/ (Accessed: 04 06 2020)

20. MBNC (2021) *Former State Dept Lead Investigator Says COVID-19 Escaped From Wuhan Lab, May Have Been Bioweapons Accident.* Available at: https://mbncnews.com/former-state-dept-lead-investigator-says-covid-19-escaped-from-wuhan-lab-may-have-been-bioweapons-accident/ (Accessed: 23 03 2021)

21. Yan, L. M., Kang, S., Guan, J., Hu, S. (2020) 'SARS-CoV-2 Is an Unrestricted Bioweapon: A Truth Revealed through Uncovering a Large-Scale, Organized Scientific Fraud', *Zenodo*, 4073131, pp.1-33.

22. Cai, J. (2020) *We can't rule out risks with Covid-19 mRNA vaccines, top Chinese health official says.* Available at: https://www.scmp.com/news/china/science/article/3115846/we-cant-rule-out-risks-covid-19-mrna-vaccines-top-chinese-health (Accessed: 19 02 2021)

23. Jakes, L. (2020) *With Beijing's Military Nearby, U.S. Sends 2 Aircraft Carriers to South China Sea.* Available at: https://www.nytimes.com/2020/07/04/us/politics/south-china-sea-aircraft-carrier.html (Accessed: 05 07 2020)

24. Farrukhzoda, N. (2020) *What they "forgot to tell us" about previous coronaviruses.* Available at: https://neiuindependent.org/17104/arts-life/opinion-what-they-forgot-to-tell-us-about-previous-coronaviruses/ (Accessed: 19 02 2021)

25. Davidson, H. (2020) *First Covid-19 case happened in November, China government records show - report.* Available at: https://www.theguardian.com/world/2020/mar/13/first-covid-19-case-happened-in-november-china-government-records-show-report (Accessed: 13 06 2020)

26. Walsh, F. (2020) *Was coronavirus here earlier than we thought?* Available at: https://www.bbc.co.uk/news/health-52935644 (Accessed: 07 06 2020)

27. Roy, M. (2021) *Five U.S. states had coronavirus infections even before first reported cases -study.* Available at: https://www.reuters.com/business/healthcare-pharmaceuticals/five-us-states-had-coronavirus-infections-even-before-first-reported-cases-study-2021-06-15/ (Accessed: 15 06 2021)

28. Basavaraju, S.V., Patton, M.E., Grimm, K., Rasheed, M.A.U., Lester, S., Mills, L., Stumpf, M., Freeman, B., Tamin, A., Harcourt, J. and Schiffer, J. (2020) 'Serologic testing of US blood donations to identify SARS-CoV-2-reactive antibodies: December 2019-January 2020', *Clinical Infectious Diseases*, 72(12), pp.1-20.

29. Amendola, A., Bianchi, S., Gori, M., Colzani, D., Canuti, M., Borghi, E., Raviglione, M.C., Zuccotti, G.V. and Tanzi, E. (2021) 'Evidence of SARS-CoV-2 RNA in an Oropharyngeal Swab Specimen, Milan, Italy, Early December 2019', *Emerging infectious diseases*, 27(2), pp.648-650.

30. Montomoli, E., Apolone, G., Manenti, A., Boeri, M., Suatoni, P., Sabia, F., Marchiano, A., Bollati, V., Pastorino, U. and Sozzi, G. (2021) 'Timeline of SARS-CoV2 spread in Italy: results from an independent serological retesting', medRxiv(Preprint)

31. Gulland, A. (2021) *Plausible evidence that Covid may have been circulating in Italy in October 2019.* Available at: https://www.telegraph.co.uk/global-health/science-and-disease/plausible-evidence-covid-may-have-circulating-italy-october/ (Accessed: 22 07 2021)

32. Machado, C. (2020) *Partículas do novo coronavírus são descobertas em amostra do esgoto de Florianópolis de novembro de 2019.* Available at: https://noticias.ufsc.br/2020/07/particulas-do-novo-coronavirus-sao-descobertas-em-amostra-do-esgoto-de-novembro-de-2019/ (Accessed: 08 07 2020)

33. Allen, N., Landauro, I. (2020) *Coronavirus traces found in March 2019 sewage sample, Spanish study shows.* Available at: https://www.reuters.com/article/us-health-coronavirus-spain-science-idUSKBN23X2HQ (Accessed: 12 03 2021)

34. Al Jazeera (2021) *'Very disappointed': WHO's COVID experts blocked from China.* Available at: https://www.aljazeera.com/news/2021/1/6/very-disappointed-whos-covid-experts-blocked-from-china (Accessed: 07 01 2021)

35. Beaumont, P. (2021) *China agrees to let in WHO team investigating Covid origins.* Available at: https://www.theguardian.com/world/2021/jan/11/china-agrees-to-let-in-who-team-investigating-covid-origins (Accessed: 11 01 2021)

36. Roberts, M. (2021) Covid: WHO says 'extremely unlikely' virus leaked from lab in China. Available at: https://www.bbc.com/news/world-asia-china-55996728 (Accessed: 09 02 2021)

37. Knapton, S. (2021) *China will have destroyed proof of Wuhan coronavirus leak, says former MI6 chief.* Available at: https://www.telegraph.co.uk/news/2021/06/03/china-will-have-destroyed-proof-wuhan-coronavirus-leak-says/ (Accessed: 03 06 2021)

38. Stahl, L. (2021) *What happened in Wuhan? Why questions still linger on the origin of the coronavirus.* Available at: https://www.cbsnews.com/news/covid-19-wuhan-origins-60-minutes-2021-03-28/ (Accessed: 14 05 2021)

39. Mendez, R. (2021) *CDC chief says lab origin of Covid is 'one possibility,' but animal host is most common for coronaviruses.* Available at: https://www.msn.com/en-us/health/medical/cdc-chief-says-lab-origin-of-covid-is-one-possibility-but-animal-host-is-most-common-for-coronaviruses/ar-BB1gUwYD (Accessed: 20 05 2021)

40. Quay, S.C. (2021) 'A Bayesian analysis concludes beyond a reasonable doubt that SARS-CoV-2 is not a natural zoonosis but instead is laboratory derived', *Zenodo*, 4477081, pp.1-193.

41. Rojo, M. and Villacorta, A. (2021) *I am convinced that the virus came out by accident from a laboratory in Wuhan.* Available at: https://www.elcomercio.es/sociedad/derrick-rose-moderna-convencido-virus-salio-laboratorio-20210625214915-nt.html (Accessed: 30 06 2021)

42. Markson, S. (2021) *World Exclusive: Footage proves bats were kept in Wuhan lab.* Available at: https://www.skynews.com.au/details/_6258639874001 (Accessed: 14 06 2021)

43. Sky News Australia (2021) *'Shocking revelations' on gain-of-function research 'raise questions' about CSIRO.* Available at: https://www.skynews.com.au/details/_6260960165001 (Accessed: 26 06 2021)

44. Xiao, X., Newman, C., Buesching, C.D., Macdonald, D.W. and Zhou, Z.M. (2021) 'Animal sales from Wuhan wet markets immediately prior to the COVID-19 pandemic', *Scientific Reports*, 11(11898), pp.1-7.

45. Kolbert, E. (2017) *Why Facts Don't Change Our Minds*. Available at: https://www.newyorker.com/magazine/2017/02/27/why-facts-dont-change-our-minds (Accessed: 31 07 2021)

46. Corman, V.M., Landt, O., Kaiser, M., Molenkamp, R., Meijer, A., Chu, D.K., Bleicker, T., Brünink, S., Schneider, J., Schmidt, M.L. and Mulders, D.G. (2020) 'Detection of 2019 novel coronavirus (2019-nCoV) by real-time RT-PCR', *Eurosurveillance*, 25(3), pp.23-30.

47. Borger, P., Malhotra, B.R., Yeadon,M. , Craig, C., McKernan, K., Steger, K., McSheehy, P., Angelova, L., Franchi, F., Binder, T., Ullrich, H., Ohashi, M., Scoglio, S., Doesburg-van Kleffens, M., Gilbert, D., Klement, R., Schruefer, R., Pieksma, B.W., Bonte, J., Carbonare, B.H.D., Corbett, K.P. and Kämmerer, U. (2021) *Review report Corman-Drosten et al. Eurosurveillance 2020.* Available at: https://cormandrostenreview.com/report/ (Accessed: 23 03 2021)

48. Public Health England (2020) 'Understanding cycle threshold (Ct) in SARS-CoV-2 RT-PCR: A guide for health protection teams', PHE gateway number: GW-1651.

49. Sands, A. (2021) WHO Information Notice for IVD Users 2020/05: Nucleic acid testing (NAT) technologies that use polymerase chain reaction (PCR) for detection of SARS-CoV-2. World Health Organisation. Available at: https://www.who.int/news/item/20-01-2021-who-information-notice-for-ivd-users-2020-05 (Accessed: 25 01 2021)

50. Cohen, A.N., Kessel, B. and Milgroom, M.G. (2020) 'Diagnosing SARS-CoV-2 infection: the danger of over-reliance on positive test results', *MedRxiv* (Preprint)

51. Rothe, C., Schunk, M., Sothmann, P., Bretzel, G., Froeschl, G., Wallrauch, C., Zimmer, T., Thiel, V., Janke, C., Guggemos, W. and Seilmaier, M. (2020) 'Transmission of 2019-nCoV infection from an asymptomatic contact in Germany', *New England Journal of Medicine*, 382(10), pp.970-971.

52. Centers for Disease Control and Prevention (2021) *COVID-19 Pandemic Planning Scenarios*. Available at: https://www.cdc.gov/coronavirus/2019-ncov/hcp/planning-scenarios.html (Accessed: 30 05 2021)

53. Cao, S., Gan, Y., Wang, C., Bachmann, M., Wei, S., Gong, J., Huang, Y., Wang, T., Li, L., Lu, K. and Jiang, H. (2020) 'Post-lockdown SARS-CoV-2 nucleic acid screening in nearly ten million residents of Wuhan, China', Nature Communications, 11(1), pp.1-7.

54. La Scola, B., Le Bideau, M., Andreani, J., Grimaldier, C., Colson, P., Gautret, P. and Raoult, D. (2020) 'Viral RNA load as determined by cell culture as a management tool for discharge of SARS-CoV-2 patients from infectious disease wards', *European Journal of Clinical Microbiology & Infectious Diseases*, 39(6), pp.1059-1061.

55. Jefferson, T., Spencer, E.A., Brassey, J. and Heneghan, C. (2020) 'Viral cultures for COVID-19 infectious potential assessment – a systematic review', *Clinical Infectious Diseases*, Available at: https://doi.org/10.1093/cid/ciaa1764 (Accessed: 12 03 2021)

56. Swedish Public Health Agency (2021) *Guidance on criteria for assessment of freedom from infection in covid-19*. Available at: https://www.folkhalsomyndigheten.se/publicerat-material/publikationsarkiv/v/vagledning-om-kriterier-for-bedomning-av-smittfrihet-vid-covid-19/ (Accessed: 21 05 2021)

57. Neil, M. (2021) 'Put to the test: use of rapid testing technologies for covid-19', *The British Medical Journal*, 372(n208)

58. Office for National Statistics (2020) *COVID-19 PCR positive test results with Cycle Threshold.* Available at: https://www.ons.gov.uk/aboutus/transparencyandgovernance/freedomofinformationfoi/covid19pcrpositivetestresultswithcyclethreshold (Accessed: 22 05 2021)

59. Mandavilli, A. (2020) *Your Coronavirus Test Is Positive. Maybe It Shouldn't Be.* Available at: https://www.nytimes.com/2020/08/29/health/coronavirus-testing.html (Accessed: 05 09 2020)

60. Centers for Disease Control and Prevention (2021) *COVID-19 Vaccine Breakthrough Case Investigation and Reporting.* Available at: https://www.cdc.gov/vaccines/covid-19/health-departments/breakthrough-cases.html (Accessed: 11 06 2021)

61. Stang, A., Robers, J., Schonert, B., Jöckel, K.H., Spelsberg, A., Keil, U. and Cullen, P. (2021) 'The performance of the SARS-CoV-2 RT-PCR test as a tool for detecting SARS-CoV-2 infection in the population', *The Journal of Infection*, 83(2), pp.237-279.

62. Heneghan, C. and Jefferson, T. (2020) *What does a case of Covid-19 really mean?* Available at: https://www.spectator.co.uk/article/what-does-a-case-of-covid-19-really-mean- (Accessed: 05 06 2021)

63. Healy, B., Khan, A., Metezai, H., Blyth, I. and Asad, H. (2021) 'The impact of false positive COVID-19 results in an area of low prevalence', Clinical Medicine, 21(1), p.e54.

64. Andrews, P. (2020) *Landmark legal ruling finds that Covid tests are not fit for purpose. So what do the MSM do? They ignore it.* Available at: https://www.rt.com/op-ed/507937-covid-pcr-test-fail/ (Accessed: 28 11 2020)

65. Willman, D. (2021) *CDC coronavirus test kits were likely contaminated, federal review confirms. Washington Post.* Available at: https://www.washingtonpost.com/investigations/cdc-coronavirus-test-kits-were-likely-contaminated-federal-review-confirms/2020/06/20/1ceb4e16-b2ef-11ea-8f56-63f38c990077_story.html (Accessed: 22 05 2021)

66. Drury, C. (2020) *Coronavirus: Randox recalls up to 750,000 test kits over safety concerns.* Available at: https://www.independent.co.uk/news/uk/home-news/coronavirus-test-kit-recall-randox-swabs-safety-concerns-a9661081.html (Accessed: 03 06 2021)

67. BBC (2021) *Covid: Secret filming exposes contamination risk at test results lab.* Available at: https://www.bbc.com/news/uk-56556806 (Accessed: 30 03 2021)

68. Ridler, F. (2020) *Five students are in quarantine after opening USED Covid nasal swab testing kits that were handed out by Birmingham council.* Available at: https://www.dailymail.co.uk/news/article-8838763/Council-hands-USED-Covid-testing-swab-kits-mistake-students.html (Accessed: 15 10 2021)

69. Cohen, J. (2020) *The coronavirus may sometimes slip its genetic material into human chromosomes.* Available at: https://www.sciencemag.org/news/2020/12/coronavirus-may-sometimes-slip-its-genetic-material-human-chromosomes-what-does-mean (Accessed: 26 02 2021)

70. Chandramouly, G., Zhao, J., McDevitt, S., Rusanov, T., Hoang, T., Borisonnik, N., Treddinick, T., Lopezcolorado, F.W., Kent, T., Siddique, L.A. and Mallon, J. (2021) 'Polθ reverse transcribes RNA and promotes RNA-templated DNA repair', *Science Advances*, 7(24), p.eabf1771.

71. Baldacci, S., Giannico, O.V., Giorgino, A., Buccoliero, G.B., Desiante, F., Fragnelli, G.R., Rizzi, R., Loconsole, D., Centrone, F., Chironna, M. and Conversano, M. (2020) '63 days detection of SARS-CoV-2 RNA from a recovered patient in Southern Italy: A Case Report', *Annali di igiene: medicina preventiva e di comunita*, 32(5), pp.590-592.

72. World Health Organisation (2020) Real-Time RT-PCR Panel for Detection2019-Novel Coronavirus: Centers for Disease Control and Prevention,Respiratory Viruses Branch, Division of Viral Diseases: Instructions for Use. Issued 24 Jan 2020.

73. Lee, S.H. (2020) 'Testing for SARS-CoV-2 in cellular components by routine nested RT-PCR followed by DNA sequencing', *International Journal of Geriatrics and Rehabilitation*, 2, pp.69-96.

74. Lintern, S. (2021) *NHS told to identify patients actually sick from Covid-19 separately to those testing positive*. Available at: https://www.independent.co.uk/news/health/coronavirus-hospitals-nhs-england-data-b1862804.html (Accessed: 10 06 2021)

75. Boyd, C. (2021) Up to 40% of 'Covid hospital patients' infected with Delta variant may have been admitted for a different illness, official figures suggest. Available at: https://www.dailymail.co.uk/news/article-9772259/40-patients-Indian-Delta-variant-admitted-hospital-reasons-Covid.html (Accessed: 10 07 2021)

76. Halliday, J. (2021) *Rapid Covid testing in England may be scaled back over false positives.* Available at: https://www.theguardian.com/world/2021/apr/15/rapid-covid-testing-in-england-may-be-scaled-back-over-false-positives (Accessed: 16 04 2021)

77. Grover, N. and Allegretti, A. (2021) *Rapid Covid tests used in mass UK programme get scathing US report.* Available at: https://www.theguardian.com/world/2021/jun/11/us-health-agency-gives-innova-lateral-flow-covid-tests-scathing-review (Accessed: 11 06 2021)

78. Mina, M.J., Peto, T.E., García-Fiñana, M., Semple, M.G. and Buchan, I.E. (2021) 'Clarifying the evidence on SARS-CoV-2 antigen rapid tests in public health responses to COVID-19', *The Lancet*, 397(10283), pp.1425-1427.

79. Zhu, N., Zhang, D., Wang, W., Li, X., Yang, B., Song, J., Zhao, X., Huang, B., Shi, W., Lu, R. and Niu, P. (2020) 'A novel coronavirus from patients with pneumonia in China', *New England journal of medicine*, 382, pp.727-733.

80. Swerling, G. (2020) *UK public 'believe coronavirus death toll 100 times higher than it really is'.* Available at: https://www.telegraph.co.uk/news/2020/08/20/uk-public-believe-coronavirus-death-toll-100-times-higher-really/ (Accessed: 21 08 2020)

81. Rayner, G. (2021) *Use of fear to control behaviour in Covid crisis was 'totalitarian', admit scientists.* Available at: https://www.telegraph.co.uk/news/2021/05/14/scientists-admit-totalitarian-use-fear-control-behaviour-covid/ (Accessed: 15 06 2021)

82. Kendrick, M. (2020) *I've signed death certificates during Covid-19. Here's why you can't trust any of the statistics on the number of victims.* Available at: https://www.rt.com/op-ed/490006-death-certificates-covid-19-do-not-trust/ (Accessed: 28 05 2020)

83. Hoenderkamp (2021) *Who has the right to decide who lives or dies?* Available at: https://www.pulsetoday.co.uk/views/coronavirus/who-has-the-right-to-decide-who-lives-or-dies/ (Accessed: 15 06 2021)

84. Craig, E. (2021) Children face just a one in 500,000 risk of dying from Covid, studies show amid growing row over whether youngsters should be given vaccines. Available at: https://www.dailymail.co.uk/news/article-9769283/Children-face-one-500-000-risk-dying-Covid-amid-row-kids-vaccinated.html (Accessed: 10 07 2021)

85. Keogh, G., Martin, A. and Ellicot, C. (2021) What IS the truth about Covid deaths? Grieving relatives along with MPs and top medics demand inquiry as families reveal MORE loved ones they believe were wrongly certified as virus victims. Available at: https://www.dailymail.co.uk/news/article-9305405/Grieving-relatives-demand-inquiry-loved-ones-wrongly-certified-virus-victims.html (Accessed: 27 02 2021)

86. Griffin, S. (2020) 'Covid-19: "Staggering number" of extra deaths in community is not explained by covid-19', *British Medical Journal*, 369(m1931)

87. Bailin, A. (2021) *Cummings' care homes claims could lead to corporate manslaughter charges.* Available at: https://www.theguardian.com/commentisfree/2021/jun/03/cummings-care-homes-corporate-manslaughter-covid (Accessed: 03 06 2021)

88. Booth, R. (2021) *Matt Hancock 'was warned of Covid care home risk in March 2020.* Available at: https://www.theguardian.com/society/2021/jun/09/matt-hancock-was-warned-of-covid-care-home-risk-in-march-2020 (Accessed: 09 06 2021)

89. Taylor, D. (2021) *Blanket 'do not resuscitate' orders imposed on English care homes, finds CQC.* Available at: https://www.theguardian.com/society/2021/mar/18/blanket-do-not-resuscitate-orders-imposed-on-english-care-homes-finds-cqc (Accessed: 03 04 2021)

90. Tapper, J. (2021) *Fury at 'do not resuscitate' notices given to Covid patients with learning disabilities.* Available at: https://www.theguardian.com/world/2021/feb/13/new-do-not-resuscitate-orders-imposed-on-covid-19-patients-with-learning-difficulties (Accessed: 03 04 2021)

91. Scobie, S. (2021) *Covid-19 and the deaths of care home residents.* Available at: https://www.nuffieldtrust.org.uk/news-item/covid-19-and-the-deaths-of-care-home-residents (Accessed: 15 06 2021)

92. The Telegraph (2021) *Medical treatment was withheld from people with learning disabilities during pandemic.* Available at: https://www.telegraph.co.uk/news/2021/06/13/medical-treatment-withheld-people-learning-disabilities-pandemic/ (Accessed: 14 06 2021)

93. Cunningham-Cook, M. (2021) *Nursing Home Industry Avoids Scrutiny for COVID-19 Deaths as Powerful Lobby Goes to Work.* Available at: https://theintercept.com/2021/02/20/covid-nursing-home-cuomo-clyburn/ (Accessed: 26 02 2021)

94. Kendrick, M. (2021) *As a GP in the NHS I witnessed first-hand the catastrophic way Matt Hancock failed the old and vulnerable in care homes.* Available at: https://www.rt.com/op-ed/526539-catastrophic-care-homes-matt-hancock/ (Accessed: 14 06 2021)

95. Preidt, R. (2020) *Study: Most N.Y. COVID Patients on Ventilators Died.* Available at: https://www.webmd.com/lung/news/20200422/most-covid-19-patients-placed-on-ventilators-died-new-york-study-shows#1 (Accessed: 05 06 2021)

96. World Health Organization (2020) Clinical management of severe acute respiratory infection (SARI) when COVID-19 disease is suspected: interim guidance, 13 March 2020 (No. WHO/2019-nCoV/clinical/2020.4)

97. Bodkin, H. (2020) *Covid death rates dropped as doctors rejected ventilators.* Available at: https://www.msn.com/en-gb/news/coronavirus/covid-death-rates-dropped-as-doctors-rejected-ventilators/ar-BB18GMUw (Accessed: 06 06 2021)

98. Ducharme, J. (2020) *Why Ventilators May Not Be Working as Well for COVID-19 Patients as Doctors Hoped.* Available at: https://time.com/5820556/ventilators-covid-19/ (Accessed: 06 06 2021)

99. Zaporowska-Stachowiak, I., Szymański, K., Oduah, M.T., Stachowiak-Szymczak, K., Łuczak, J. and Sopata, M. (2019) 'Midazolam: safety of use in palliative care: a systematic critical review', *Biomedicine & Pharmacotherapy*, 114, pp.1-7.

100. Chen, T.Y., Winkelman, J.W., Mao, W.C., Liu, C.L., Hsu, C.Y. and Wu, C.S. (2018) 'The use of benzodiazepine receptor agonists and the risk of hospitalization for pneumonia: a nationwide population-based nested case-control study', *Chest*, 153(1), pp.161-171.

101. Adams, S. (2021) *Did care homes use powerful sedative to speed covid deaths?* Available at: https://www.msn.com/en-xl/news/other/did-care-homes-use-powerful-sedative-to-speed-covid-deaths/ar-BB16COBW (Accessed: 06 06 2021)

102. The Telegraph Investigations Team (2021) *NHS made secret pandemic plan to deny care to elderly.* Available at: https://www.telegraph.co.uk/news/2021/07/30/nhs-made-secret-pandemic-plan-deny-care-elderly/ (Accessed: 31 07 2021)

103. Lovelace Jr, B. and Higgins-Dunn, N. (2020) *WHO says coronavirus death rate is 3.4% globally, higher than previously thought. CNBC.* Available at: https://www.cnbc.com/2020/03/03/who-says-coronavirus-death-rate-is-3point4percent-globally-higher-than-previously-thought.html (Accessed: 15 04 2020)

104. Ioannidis, J.P.A. (2020) *Bulletin of the World Health Organization: Infection fatality rate of COVID-19 inferred from seroprevalence data.* Available at: https://www.who.int/bulletin/volumes/99/1/20-265892/en/ (Accessed: 06 06 2021)

105. Ioannidis, J.P., Axfors, C. and Contopoulos-Ioannidis, D.G. (2020) 'Population-level COVID-19 mortality risk for non-elderly individuals overall and for non-elderly individuals without underlying diseases in pandemic epicenters', *Environmental Research*, 188(109890).

106. Brown, R.B. (2020) 'Public health lessons learned from biases in coronavirus mortality overestimation', *Disaster Medicine and Public Health Preparedness,* 14(3), pp.364-371.

107. Centers for Disease Control and Prevention (2021) *COVID-19 Pandemic Planning Scenarios*. Available at: https://www.cdc.gov/coronavirus/2019-ncov/hcp/planning-scenarios.html (Accessed: 15 07 2021)

108. Ioannidis, J.P. (2021) 'Reconciling estimates of global spread and infection fatality rates of COVID-19: An overview of systematic evaluations', *European journal of clinical investigation*, 51(5), p.e13554.

109. Brazeau, N., Verity, R., Jenks, S., Fu, H., Whittaker, C., Winskill, P., Dorigatti, I., Walker, P., Riley, S., Schnekenberg, R.P. and Heltgebaum, H. (2020) *Report 34: COVID-19 infection fatality ratio: estimates from seroprevalence.* Imperial College London.

110. Colton, E. (2020) *Minnesota lawmakers say coronavirus deaths could be inflated by 40% after reviewing death certificates.* Available at: https://www.washingtonexaminer.com/news/coronavirus-death-certificates-minnesota-inflated (Accessed: 23 05 2021)

111. Knapton, S. (2021) *Nearly 40 per cent of recent Covid victims died primarily of other conditions.* Available at: https://www.telegraph.co.uk/news/2021/06/02/nearly-40-per-cent-recent-covid-victims-died-primarily-conditions/amp (Accessed: 04 06 2021)

112. Triggle, N. (2021) *Covid: 2020 saw most excess deaths since World War Two.* Available at: https://www.bbc.com/news/uk-55631693 (Accessed: 13 01 2021)

113. Appleby, J. (2021) 'UK deaths in 2020: how do they compare with previous years?', *The British Medical Journal*, 373(n896).

114. Public Health England (2018) *A review of recent trends in mortality in England* (GW-686).

115. Office for National Statistics (2021) *Deaths in the UK from 1990 to 2020.* Available at: https://www.ons.gov.uk/aboutus/transparencyandgovernance/freedomofinformationfoi/death sintheukfrom1990to2020?fbclid=IwAR1w7oDyRgUB5wB8wWLKh33HM6c3Axr07qeUblBpD GpVCX7Q551wKzm7uiQ (Accessed: 15 07 2021)

116. Department of Health (2010) KH03: Average daily number of available beds, by sector, England, 1987-88 to 2009-10.

117. NHS England (2021) KH03: Average Daily Available and Occupied Beds Time series.

118. Youle, E. (2021) *Revealed: What Really Happened In The Nightingales.* The Huffington Post. Available at: https://www.huffingtonpost.co.uk/entry/nightingale-hospitals-covid-patient-numbers_uk_605a0dd6c5b6cebf58d220eb (Accessed: 02 07 2021)

119. Lydall, R. (2016) *Revealed: 30,000 patients left waiting in ambulances outside London A&Es last year.* Available at: https://www.standard.co.uk/news/health/revealed-30-000-patients-left-waiting-in-ambulances-outside-london-a-es-last-year-a3259881.html (Accessed: 02 11 2020)

120. Halle, M. and Small, N. (2015) *Picture that shames Britain: Patients queue in corridor 'for hours' just to SIGN IN for A&E.* Available at: https://www.mirror.co.uk/news/uk-news/nhs-whistleblower-fears-patients-die-6875670 (Accessed: 30 12 2020)

121. Deadline News Agency (2015) *Teen dies after ambulance takes almost 30 minutes to reach crash scene.* Available at: https://www.deadlinenews.co.uk/2015/02/05/teen-dies-after-ambulance-takes-almost-30-minutes-to-reach-crash-scene/ (Accessed: 09 01 2021)

122. Meikle, J. (2015) *Ambulance crew who left body on floor 'thought it was normal practice'.* Available at: https://www.theguardian.com/society/2015/jan/14/ambulance-staff-dead-body-floor-common-practice-inquest (Accessed: 17 06 2021)

123. Smith, M. (2016) *A huge number of ambulances were caught on video queuing at Wales' largest A&E.* Available at: https://www.walesonline.co.uk/news/health/huge-number-ambulances-were-caught-12207962 (Accessed: 31 12 2020)

124. Bulman, M. (2017) *Number of NHS patients waiting more than 12 hours on hospital trolleys rises 6,000%, figures show.* Available at: https://www.independent.co.uk/news/uk/home-news/nhs-patients-trolleys-wait-12-hours-more-rise-6000-cent-hospitals-british-medical-association-a7757016.html (29 12 2020)

125. Hagger, A. (2017) *Grandmother, 94, 'could have died' after being left waiting SEVEN hours for ambulance.* Available at: https://www.express.co.uk/news/uk/827903/Patient-waiting-ambulance-times-grandmother-fall (Accessed: 09 01 2021)

126. Yarwood, S. (2017) *Pensioner who bled to death after cutting his head open was 'let down by the NHS', says sister.* Available at: https://www.manchestereveningnews.co.uk/news/greater-manchester-news/pensioner-bled-death-after-paramedics-12508001 (Accessed: 09 01 2021)

127. Willis, A. (2017) *Screaming on the bedroom floor I dialled 999 but was refused an ambulance.* Available at: https://metro.co.uk/2017/03/12/screaming-on-the-bedroom-floor-i-dialled-999-but-was-refused-an-ambulance-6461761/ (Accessed: 09 01 2021)

128. Triggle, N. (2018) *Patients 'dying in hospital corridors'.* Available at: https://www.bbc.co.uk/news/health-42572116 (Accessed: 29 12 2020)

129. Matthews-King, A. (2018) *NHS winter crisis officially worst on record and patients still suffering, final figures show.* Available at: https://www.independent.co.uk/news/health/nhs-winter-crisis-worst-record-patient-deaths-ambulance-waits-beds-jeremy-hunt-a8259881.html (Accessed: 09 01 2021)

130. Anandaciva, S. (2018) *Hidden from the targets: how long are patients waiting for NHS care?* Available at: https://www.kingsfund.org.uk/blog/2018/02/hidden-targets-patients-waiting-nhs-care (Accessed: 29 12 2020)

131. Neville, S. (2019) *NHS doctor shortages cannot be filled, think-tanks warn.* Available at: https://www.ft.com/content/e265604c-4a80-11e9-bbc9-6917dce3dc62 (Accessed: 31 12 2020)

132. Borland, S. (2019) So THAT'S why you can't get a doctor: A record 138 surgeries closed down last year as hundreds of GPs quit leaving millions of patients affected. Available at: https://www.dailymail.co.uk/health/article-7087309/Record-138-surgeries-closed-year-GPs-early-retirement-change-career.html (Accessed: 31 12 2020)

133. Illman, J. (2019) *Revealed: 'At least 40 patients died or harmed' after ambulance delays.* Available at: https://www.hsj.co.uk/emergency-care/revealed-at-least-40-patients-died-or-harmed-after-ambulance-delays/7021492.article (Accessed: 30 12 2020)

134. Pym, H. (2020) *Coronavirus: England death count review reduces UK toll by 5,000.* Available at: https://www.bbc.com/news/health-53722711 (Accessed: 16 07 2021)

135. Department of Health and Social Care (2020) *New UK-wide methodology agreed to record COVID-19 death.* Available at: https://www.gov.uk/government/news/new-uk-wide-methodology-agreed-to-record-covid-19-deaths (Accessed: 16 07 2021)

136. Slater, T.A., Straw, S., Drozd, M., Kamalathasan, S., Cowley, A. and Witte, K.K. (2020) 'Dying 'due to' or 'with' COVID-19: a cause of death analysis in hospitalised patients', *Clinical Medicine*, 20(5), pp.e189-190.

137. Roulson, J.A., Benbow, E.W. and Hasleton, P.S. (2005) Discrepancies between clinical and autopsy diagnosis and the value of post mortem histology; a meta-analysis and review. *Histopathology,* 47(6), pp.551-559.

138. Public Health England (2020) *High consequence infectious diseases (HCID)*. Available at: https://www.gov.uk/guidance/high-consequence-infectious-diseases-hcid (Accessed: 06 08 2021)

139. YouTube (2020) Bill Gates said that the "Final Solution" to end coronavirus disease is the vaccine. Available at: https://www.youtube.com/watch?v=mWK4i9j-aUc (Accessed: 14 03 2021)

140. Goodman, J. and Carmichael, F. (2020) *Coronavirus: Bill Gates 'microchip' conspiracy theory and other vaccine claims fact-checked.* Available at: https://www.bbc.co.uk/news/52847648 (Accessed: 30 05 2020)

141. Goodman, J. and Carmichael, F. (2020) *Coronavirus: False and misleading claims about vaccines debunked.* Available at: https://www.bbc.co.uk/news/53525002 (Accessed: 27 07 2020)

142. Tobitt, C. (2021) Journalists claim alternative Covid-19 news has been 'censored' to create 'one official narrative'. Available at: https://www.pressgazette.co.uk/journalists-claim-alternative-covid-19-news-censorship-create-one-official-narrative (Accessed: 27 07 2021)

143. Gyles, C. (2015) 'Skeptical of medical science reports?', *The Canadian Veterinary Journal*, 56(10), pp.1011-1012.

144. Smith, R. (2021) *Time to assume that health research is fraudulent until proven otherwise?* Available at: https://blogs.bmj.com/bmj/2021/07/05/time-to-assume-that-health-research-is-fraudulent-until-proved-otherwise/ (Accessed: 10 07 2021)

145. Compton, W.M., Conway, K.P., Stinson, F.S., Colliver, J.D. and Grant, B.F. (2005) 'Prevalence, correlates, and comorbidity of DSM-IV antisocial personality syndromes and alcohol and specific drug use disorders in the United States: results from the national epidemiologic survey on alcohol and related conditions', *Journal of Clinical Psychiatry*, 66(6), pp.677-685.

146. Babiak, P., Neumann, C. S. and Hare, R. D. (2010) 'Corporate psychopathy: Talking the walk.', *Behavioural Sciences and the Law*, 28(2), pp.174-193.

147. Bourke, J. (2019) *Some surgeons may be psychopaths - but that's no bad thing.* Available at: https://www.prospectmagazine.co.uk/magazine/two-new-books-explore-how-surgeons-must-be-resolute-and-merciless (Accessed: 25 09 2019)

148. Boddy, C. R. (2016) 'Psychopathy screening for public leadership', *International Journal of Public Leadership*, 12(4), pp.254-274.

149. Allison, G. (2020) *77 Brigade is countering Covid misinformation.* Available at: https://ukdefencejournal.org.uk/77-brigade-is-countering-covid-misinformation/ (Accessed: 13 07 2021)

150. Davis, I. (2021) *Buying a Single Version of the Truth.* Available at: https://www.ukcolumn.org/article/buying-a-single-version-of-the-truth (Accessed: 13 07 2021)

151. Sweney, M. (2020) *UK advertisers pulled more than £1.1bn spend during Covid lockdown.* Available at: https://www.theguardian.com/media/2020/aug/04/uk-advertisers-spend-covid-lockdown-coronavirus (Accessed: 13 07 2021)

152. Llamas, M. (2020) *Pfizer.* Available at: https://www.drugwatch.com/manufacturers/pfizer/ (Accessed: 14 03 2021)

153. Thomas, J. (2021) *Hereford GP refuses Covid jab but says she's not an 'anti-vaxxer'.* Available at: https://www.herefordtimes.com/news/19140280.hereford-gp-refuses-covid-jab-says-not-anti-vaxxer/ (Accessed: 14 03 2021)

154. Kendrick, M. (2020) As a doctor, people ask me if it's safe to take a new Covid vaccine. Given that criticism is risky, here's my very careful answer. Available at: https://www.rt.com/op-ed/507587-covid19-vaccine-safe-coronavirus/ (Accessed: 25 11 2020)

155. Cairns News (2020) *Scientists, doctors won't take the mRNA COVID vaccines: Why should you?* Available at: https://cairnsnews.org/2020/12/15/scientists-doctors-wont-take-the-mrna-covid-vaccines-why-should-you/ (Accessed: 14 03 2021)

156. Good Jobs First (2021) *Violation Tracker: Astra Zeneca.* Available at: https://violationtracker.goodjobsfirst.org/prog.php?parent=astrazeneca (Accessed: 29 06 2021)

157. Good Jobs First (2021) *Violation Tracker: Johnson and Johnson.* Available at: https://violationtracker.goodjobsfirst.org/prog.php?parent=johnson-and-johnson (Accessed: 29 06 2021)

158. Good Jobs First (2021) *Violation Tracker: Pfizer.* Available at: https://violationtracker.goodjobsfirst.org/prog.php?parent=pfizer (Accessed: 29 06 2021)

159. Competition and Markets Authority (2016) *CMA fines Pfizer and Flynn £90 million for drug price hike to NHS.* Available at: https://www.gov.uk/government/news/cma-fines-pfizer-and-flynn-90-million-for-drug-price-hike-to-nhs (Accessed: 29 06 2021)

160. Garde, D. (2016) *Ego, ambition, and turmoil: Inside one of biotech's most secretive startups.* Available at: https://www.statnews.com/2016/09/13/moderna-therapeutics-biotech-mrna/ (Accessed: 06 07 2021)

161. Saigol, L. (2021) *AstraZeneca sold its stake in Moderna for more than $1 billion, as it looks to develop its own pipeline of drugs.* Available at: https://www.marketwatch.com/story/astrazeneca-sold-its-stake-in-moderna-for-more-than-1-billion-last-year-11614606815 (Accessed: 06 07 2021)

162. Angel, J. and Deardon, N. (2021) The Horrible History of Big Pharma: Why we can't leave pharmaceutical corporations in the driving seat of the Covid-19 response. London: Global Justice Now.

163. Hawthorne, J. (2020) *Is Novavax a Ticking Time Bomb for Investors?* Available at: https://www.fool.com/investing/2020/11/14/is-novavax-a-ticking-time-bomb-for-investors/ (Accessed: 09 07 2021)

164. Thomas, K. and Twohey, M. (2021) *How a Struggling Company Won $1.6 Billion to Make a Coronavirus Vaccine.* Available at: https://www.nytimes.com/2020/07/16/health/coronavirus-vaccine-novavax.html (Accessed: 09 07 2021)

165. Yahoo Finance (2021) *Novavax, Inc.* Available at: https://finance.yahoo.com/quote/NVAX (Accessed: 09 07 2021)

166. Dyer, C. (2021) 'Covid-19: Hancock's failure to publish contracts was unlawful', *The British Medical Journal*, 372(n511).

167. Lawrence, F. (2020) *Hancock's former neighbour won Covid test kit work after WhatsApp message.* Available at: https://www.theguardian.com/world/2020/nov/26/matt-hancock-former-neighbour-won-covid-test-kit-contract-after-whatsapp-message (Accessed: 28 11 2020)

168. Owen, G. (2021) Inside the plot to expose Matt Hancock's affair: Friends talk of secret camera hidden by Chinese... or No10. In fact it was footage from his office CCTV and a whistleblower in his own department. Available at: https://www.dailymail.co.uk/news/article-9728843/Matt-Hancocks-affair-footage-office-CCTV-reveals-GLEN-OWEN.html (Accessed: 06 07 2021)

169. Jenkins, S. (2021) *Ten years in jail – Matt Hancock's threat is the distress call of a minister losing his grip.* Available at: https://www.theguardian.com/commentisfree/2021/feb/11/ten-years-in-jail-matt-hancocks-threat-is-the-distress-call-of-a-minister-losing-his-grip (Accessed: 06 07 2021)

170. Sherwood, H. (2019) *Sexism, vandalism and bullying: inside the Boris Johnson-era Bullingdon Club.* Available at: https://www.theguardian.com/politics/2019/jul/07/oxford-bullingdon-club-boris-johnson-sexism-violence-bullying-culture (Accessed: 06 07 2021)

171. Sparrow, A. (2011) *Bullingdon Club antics were nothing like the riots, says Cameron.* Available at: https://www.theguardian.com/politics/2011/sep/02/bullingdon-club-david-cameron-riots (Accessed: 17 07 2021)

172. BBC (2018) Boris Johnson's unused water cannon sold for scrap at £300k loss. Available at: https://www.bbc.co.uk/news/uk-england-london-46258584 (Accessed: 06 07 2021)

173. Drewett, Z. (2019) *Boris Johnson broke law with parliament suspension, Supreme Court rules.* Available at: https://metro.co.uk/2019/09/24/boris-johnson-broke-law-parliament-suspension-supreme-court-rules-10797329/ (Accessed: 06 07 2021)

174. O' Donoghue, D. (2020) *Boris Johnson guilty of 'gross breach of ministerial code' after admission Brexit plan breaks the law.* Available at: https://www.eveningexpress.co.uk/fp/news/uk/boris-johnson-guilty-of-gross-breach-of-ministerial-code-after-admission-brexit-plan-breaks-the-law/ (Accessed: 06 07 2021)

175. Sky News (2021) Boris Johnson was 'unwise' to allow flat refurbishment 'without more rigorous regard for how this would be funded', report finds. Available at: https://news.sky.com/story/boris-johnson-was-unwise-to-allow-flat-refurbishment-without-more-rigorous-regard-for-how-this-would-be-funded-12319292 (Accessed: 16 07 2021)

176. Smith, B. (2021) *PM blocks new standards adviser from launching own investigations.* Available at: https://www.civilserviceworld.com/news/article/pm-appoints-adviser-on-ministerial-conduct-but-wont-give-green-light-to-launch-investigations (Accessed: 16 07 2021)

177. Syal, R. (2021) *Ex-Bullingdon Club member appointed to Whitehall's sleaze watchdog.* Available at: https://www.theguardian.com/politics/2021/jul/15/ex-bullingdon-club-member-appointed-to-whitehalls-sleaze-watchdog (Accessed: 16 07 2021)

178. Conn, D., Pegg, D., Evans, R., Garside, J. and Lawrence, F. (2020) *'Chumocracy': how Covid revealed the new shape of the Tory establishment.* Available at: 'https://www.theguardian.com/world/2020/nov/15/chumocracy-covid-revealed-shape-tory-establishment (Accessed: 06 07 2021)

179. Thacker, P.D. (2020) 'Conflicts of interest among the UK government's covid-19 advisers', *The British Medical Journal*, 371(m4716).

180. University Philanthropy (2020) *An analysis of university giving by the Bill & Melinda Gates Foundation.* Available at: https://www.universityphilanthropy.com/bill-and-melinda-gates-foundation-funding (Accessed: 23 08 2021)

181. The Bill and Melinda Gates Foundation (2021) *Bill and Melinda Gates Pledge $10 Billion in Call for Decade of Vaccines.* Available at: https://www.gatesfoundation.org/ideas/media-center/press-releases/2010/01/bill-and-melinda-gates-pledge-$10-billion-in-call-for-decade-of-vaccines (Accessed: 17 07 2021)

182. Cheney, C. (2021) *Gates Foundation COVID-19 commitment reaches $1.75B with latest pledge.* Available at: https://www.devex.com/news/gates-foundation-covid-19-commitment-reaches-1-75b-with-latest-pledge-98739 (Accessed: 17 07 2021)

183. Medicines and Healthcare Products Regulatory Agency (2017) *MHRA awarded over £980,000 for collaboration with the Bill and Melinda Gates Foundation and the World Health Organisation.* Available at: https://www.gov.uk/government/news/mhra-awarded-over-980000-for-collaboration-with-the-bill-and-melinda-gates-foundation-and-the-world-health-organisation (Accessed: 29 06 2021)

184. Evans, R. and Bosely, S. (2004) *The drugs industry and its watchdog: a relationship too close for comfort?* Available at: https://www.theguardian.com/society/2004/oct/04/health.businessofresearch1 (Accessed: 27 06 2021)

185. Schwab, T. (2020) *Journalism's Gate Keepers.* Available at: https://www.cjr.org/criticism/gates-foundation-journalism-funding.php (Accessed: 17 07 2021)

186. Khazan, O. (2020) *Inside the Mind of an Anti-vaxxer.* Available at: https://www.theatlantic.com/health/archive/2020/10/how-change-mind-anti-vaxxer/616722/ (Accessed: 14 03 2021)

187. Lewis, T. (2021) *CDC Says Vaccinated People Do Not Need to Wear Masks in Most Settings.* Available at: https://www.scientificamerican.com/article/cdc-says-vaccinated-people-do-not-need-to-wear-masks-in-most-settings/ (Accessed: 14 05 2021)

188. National Instiues of Health (2021) Study to Describe the Safety, Tolerability, Immunogenicity, and Efficacy of RNA Vaccine Candidates Against COVID-19 in Healthy Individuals. Available at: https://clinicaltrials.gov/ct2/show/NCT04368728 (Accessed: 29 07 2021)

189. DW News (2020) *Anti-vaxxers should forgo ventilators, German doctor says.* Available at:
https://www.dw.com/en/anti-vaxxers-should-forgo-ventilators-german-doctor-says/a-
55996805 (Accessed: 17 07 2021)

190. BBC News (2020) *Coronavirus: Spain to keep register of those who refuse Covid vaccine.*
Available at: https://www.bbc.co.uk/news/world-europe-55471282 (Accessed: 29 12 2020)

191. RT News (2021) Unvaccinated citizens' names should be DISCLOSED, new proposal by
Israeli PM suggests amid slowdown in immunization campaign. Available at:
https://www.rt.com/news/515621-netanyahu-disclose-names-vaccination/ (Accessed: 16 02
2021)

192. Yale Law School (2008) *Nuremberg Code.* Available at:
https://avalon.law.yale.edu/imt/nurecode.asp (Accessed: 14 05 2021)

193. UNESCO (2005) *Universal Declaration on Bioethics and Human Rights.* Available at:
http://portal.unesco.org/en/ev.php-
URL_ID=31058&URL_DO=DO_TOPIC&URL_SECTION=201.html (Accessed: 14 05 2021)

194. Madani, D. (2021) *Texas Gov. Greg Abbott bans government-mandated 'vaccine
passports'. NBC News.* Available at: https://www.nbcnews.com/news/us-news/texas-gov-
greg-abbott-bans-government-mandated-vaccine-passports-n1263170 (Accessed: 12 06
2021)

195. Aitken, V. (2021) *Scots care home resident 'held down and vaccinated against her will' as
two workers suspended.* Available at: https://www.dailyrecord.co.uk/news/scottish-
news/scots-care-home-resident-held-23937350 (Accessed: 05 05 2021)

196. Mommaerts, J. L. (2021) 'COVID Vaccination Studies: From Double-Blind to Hardly-
Blind?', The British Medical Journal, 371(m4924).

197. The College of Physicians of Philadelphia (2018) *Vaccine Development, Testing, and Regulation.* Available at: https://www.historyofvaccines.org/content/articles/vaccine-development-testing-and-regulation (Accessed: 14 06 2020)

198. RT News (2021) 'Chilling Big Tech censorship': YouTube accused of terminating TalkRADIO channel, allegedly for airing views of lockdown skeptics. Available at: https://www.rt.com/uk/511559-youtube-removes-talkradio-lockdown/ (Accessed: 25 01 2021)

199. Feuer, W. (2021) *Facebook trying to censor posts from COVID-19 vaccine skeptics: report.* Available at: https://nypost.com/2021/05/25/facebook-trying-to-censor-covid-19-vaccine-skeptics-report/ (Accessed: 29 05 2021)

200. Need to Know News (2021) *Could Dr. Shiva's Case Against Twitter Censorship End Big Tech's Immunity from Lawsuits?* Available at: https://needtoknow.news/2021/05/could-dr-shivas-case-against-twitter-censorship-end-big-techs-immunity-from-lawsuits/ (Accessed: 18 05 2021)

201. Bhattacharya, J. and Kulldorff, M. (2021) *Facebook is silencing debate on lockdown.* Available at: https://www.spiked-online.com/2021/02/15/facebook-is-silencing-debate-on-lockdown/ (Accessed: 21 02 2021)

202. Wulfsohn, J.A. (2021) *Facebook whistleblower fired after leaking 'vaccine hesitancy' censorship documents to Project Veritas.* Available at: https://www.foxnews.com/media/facebook-whistleblower-morgan-kahmann-fired-project-veritas (Accessed: 29 05 2021)

203. World Health Organisation (2020) What is 'herd immunity'? Available at: https://www.who.int/news-room/q-a-detail/herd-immunity-lockdowns-and-covid-19 (Accessed: 25 05 2021)

204. Yaqinuddin, A. (2020) 'Cross-immunity between respiratory coronaviruses may limit COVID-19 fatalities', *Medical Hypotheses*, 144(110049), pp.1-3.

205. Majdoubi, A., Michalski, C., O'Connell, S.E., Dada, S., Narpala, S., Gelinas, J., Mehta, D., Cheung, C., Winkler, D.F., Basappa, M. and Liu, A.C. (2020) 'A majority of uninfected adults show preexisting antibody reactivity against SARS-CoV-2', *JCI Insight*, 6(8), pp.1-10.

206. Steel, K. and Hill, T. (2021) Coronavirus (COVID-19) Infection Survey, antibody and vaccination data, UK: 7 July 2021. Office for National Statistics.

207. Costello, A. (2020) *The government's secret science group has a shocking lack of expertise.* Available at: https://www.theguardian.com/commentisfree/2020/apr/27/gaps-sage-scientific-body-scientists-medical (Accessed: 19 07 2021)

208. Doshi, P. (2020) 'Covid-19: Do many people have pre-existing immunity', *The British Medical Journal*, 375(m3563).

209. Ivanova, E.N., Devlin, J.C., Buus, T.B., Koide, A., Cornelius, A., Samanovic, M.I., Herrera, A., Zhang, C., Desvignes, L., Odum, N. and Ulrich, R. (2021) 'Discrete immune response signature to SARS-CoV-2 mRNA vaccination versus infection', medRxiv (Preprint)

210. Nielsen, S.S., Vibholm, L.K., Monrad, I., Olesen, R., Frattari, G.S., Pahus, M.H., Højen, J.F., Gunst, J.D., Erikstrup, C., Holleufer, A. and Hartmann, R. (2021) 'SARS-CoV-2 elicits robust adaptive immune responses regardless of disease severity', *EBioMedicine*, 68(103410), pp.2-11.

211. Wiedermann, U., Garner-Spitzer, E. and Wagner, A. (2016) 'Primary vaccine failure to routine vaccines: why and what to do?', Human Vaccines & Immunotherapeutics, 12(1), pp.239-243.

212. Turner, J.S., Kim, W., Kalaidina, E., Goss, C.W., Rauseo, A.M., Schmitz, A.J., Hansen, L., Haile, A., Klebert, M.K., Pusic, I. and O'Halloran, J.A. (2021) 'SARS-CoV-2 infection induces long-lived bone marrow plasma cells in humans', Nature (Accelerated preview), pp.1-5

213. Callaway, E. (2021) *Had COVID? You'll probably make antibodies for a lifetime.* Available at: https://www.nature.com/articles/d41586-021-01442-9 (Accessed: 28 05 2021)

214. Rosenburg, D. (2021) *Natural infection vs vaccination: Which gives more protection?* Available at: https://www.israelnationalnews.com/News/News.aspx/309762 (Accessed: 14 07 2021)

215. Office for National Statistics (2021) *Coronavirus (COVID-19) latest insights.* Available at: https://www.ons.gov.uk/peoplepopulationandcommunity/healthandsocialcare/conditionsand diseases/articles/coronaviruscovid19/latestinsights (Accessed: 06 08 2021)

216. Knapton, S. (2021) *Delta variant has wrecked hopes of herd immunity, warn scientists.* Available at: https://www.telegraph.co.uk/news/2021/08/10/delta-variant-has-wrecked-hopes-herd-immunity-warn-scientists/ (Accessed: 13 08 2021)

217. MHRA (2021) *REG 174 Information for UK Healthcare Professionals.* (Astra Zeneca - no report reference given)

218. MHRA (2021) *REG 174 Information for UK Healthcare Professionals.* Ref: SPC BNT162 UK 12_0

219. MHRA (2021) Information for Healthcare Professionals on Pfizer/BioNTech COVID-19 vaccine: Regulation 174 Information for UK healthcare professionals. Available at: https://www.gov.uk/government/publications/regulatory-approval-of-pfizer-biontech-vaccine-for-covid-19/information-for-healthcare-professionals-on-pfizerbiontech-covid-19-vaccine (Accessed: 29 06 2021)

220. MHRA (2021) *Reg 174 Information for UK Recipients* (revised 24 06 2021).

221. MHRA (2021) *Summary of Product Characteristics for COVID-19 Vaccine Moderna.* Available at: https://www.gov.uk/government/publications/regulatory-approval-of-covid-19-vaccine-moderna/information-for-healthcare-professionals-on-covid-19-vaccine-modernaSummary of Product Characteristics for COVID-19 Vaccine Moderna (Accessed: 29 06 2021)

222. MHRA (2021) *Summary of Product Characteristics for COVID-19 Vaccine Janssen.* Available at: https://www.gov.uk/government/publications/regulatory-approval-of-covid-19-vaccine-janssen/summary-of-product-characteristics-for-covid-19-vaccine-janssen (Accessed: 29 06 2021)

223. Public Health England (2017) '9: Surveillance and monitoring for vaccine safety', In: Ramsay, Dr M. (ed.) *The Green Book: Immunisation Against Infectious Diseases.*

224. Belton, K.J., Lewis, S.C., Payne, S., Rawlins, M.D. and Wood, S.M. (1995) 'Attitudinal survey of adverse drug reaction reporting by medical practitioners in the United Kingdom', *British Journal of Clinical Pharmacology*, 39(3), pp.223-226.

225. Lopez-Gonzalez, E., Herdeiro, M.T. and Figueiras, A. (2009) 'Determinants of under-reporting of adverse drug reactions', Drug Safety, 32(1), pp.19-31.

226. Al Dwelk, R., Yaya, S., Stacey, D. and Kohen, D. (2020) 'Patients' experiences on adverse drug reactions reporting: a qualitative study', *European Journal of Clinical Pharmacology*, 76(12), pp.1723-1730.

227. Amedome, S.N. and Dadson, B.A. (2017) 'Pharmacovigilance practices: Knowledge and attitudes among the healthcare professionals at the Volta Regional hospital of Ghana', *Journal of Pharmacovigilance*, 5(3), p.1000229.

228. Chaplin, S. (2019) 'Monitoring drug safety: is the Yellow Card Scheme struggling?', *Prescriber*, 30(9), pp.32-34.

229. MHRA (2019) *Yellow Card: please help to reverse the decline in reporting of suspected adverse drug reactions.* Available at: https://www.gov.uk/drug-safety-update/yellow-card-please-help-to-reverse-the-decline-in-reporting-of-suspected-adverse-drug-reactions (Accessed: 28 06 2021)

230. Hazell, L. and Shakir, S.A. (2006) 'Under-reporting of adverse drug reactions', *Drug safety*, 29(5), pp.385-396.

231. Stone, J. (2021) Rapid Response: Deep concern over vaccination safety. *The British Medical Journal*, 372(n393).

232. Lazarus, R., Klompas, M. and Bernstein, S. (2010) Electronic Support for Public Health–Vaccine Adverse Event Reporting System (ESP: VAERS). Grant ID: R18 HS 017045.

233. Walach, H., Klement, R.J. and Aukema, W. (2021) 'The Safety of COVID-19 Vaccinations - We Should Rethink the Policy', *Vaccines*, 9(7), pp.1-8.

234. MHRA (2021) *Coronavirus vaccine - weekly summary of Yellow Card reporting.* Available at: https://www.gov.uk/government/publications/coronavirus-covid-19-vaccine-adverse-reactions/coronavirus-vaccine-summary-of-yellow-card-reporting#annex-1-vaccine-analysis-print (Accessed: 17 07 2021)

235. Wise, J. (2021) 'Covid-19: Vaccines journal retracts controversial paper after editorial board members quit', *The British Medical Journal*, 374(n1726).

236. Weaver, M. (2021) *Not enough evidence to back Covid jabs for children, says UK expert.* Available at: http://web.archive.org/web/20210701090721/https://www.theguardian.com/society/2021/jul/01/not-enough-evidence-to-back-covid-jabs-for-children-says-uk-expert (Accessed: 01 07 2021)

237. Faust, J. S., Mayes, K. D. and Gounder, C. (2021) *Covid Is a Greater Risk to Young People Than the Vaccines.* The New York Times. Available at: https://www.nytimes.com/2021/07/04/opinion/covid-vaccine-kids-risks.html (Accessed: 10 07 2021)

238. CDC (2021) United States Department of Health and Human Services (DHHS), Public Health Service (PHS), Centers for Disease Control (CDC) / Food and Drug Administration (FDA), Vaccine Adverse Event Reporting System (VAERS) 1990 - 07/02/2021, CDC WONDER On-line Database. Available at: http://wonder.cdc.gov/vaers.html (Accessed: 10 07 2021)

239. Gardner, B.(2021) *Exclusive: Children being given vaccine as councils 'go rogue'.* Available at: https://www.telegraph.co.uk/news/2021/07/02/children-vaccinated-councils-go-rogue/ (Accessed: 03 07 2021)

240. Jones, R., Fryer, A., Sikora, A., Dalgleish, A., Ennos, R., Brookes, A.J., Lee, J.A., Mordue, A., Evans, E., Loudon, M., Quinn, G., Maidment, C.G., Singh, K., Jones, P., Young, H., Critchley, D., Kanthan, P., Carnwath, T., McBride, S., Westwood, H., Bell, M.A., Donegan, D.L.M., Mukherjee, D., Craig, C., Chilton, C.P., Lawrie, T., Lester, J., Flack, J., Williams, S., Mushet, G., Hinton, A., Corcoran, E., Black, A., Peers, C., Chiesa, M., Thomas, N., Sadler, M. and Bridges, I. (2021) *Open Letter from UK doctors: Safety and Ethical Concerns Surrounding COVID19 Vaccination in Children to Dr June Raine, Chief Executive, MHRA.*

241. Bruno, R., McCullough, P.A., i Vila, T.F., Henrion-Caude, A., García-Gasca, T., Zaitzeva, G.P., Priester, S., Albarracín, M.J.M., Sousa-Escandon, A., Mirones, F.L. and Cifre, B.P. (2021) *SARS-CoV-2 mass vaccination: Urgent questions on vaccine safety that demand answers from international health agencies, regulatory authorities, governments and vaccine developers.*

242. Olliaro, P., Torreele, E. and Vaillant, M. (2021) 'COVID-19 vaccine efficacy and effectiveness—the elephant(not) in the room', *The Lancet Microbe*, 2(7), pp.e279-280

243. Correia, L.C. and Matias, D. (2021) 'COVID-19 vaccines: effectiveness and number needed to treat', *The Lancet Microbe*, 2(7), pp.e281

244. Olliaro, P., Torreele, E. and Vaillant, M. (2021) 'COVID-19 vaccines: effectiveness and number needed to treat–Authors' reply', *The Lancet Microbe*, 2(7), p. e282.

245. Brown, R. B. (2021) 'Outcome reporting bias in COVID-19 mRNA vaccine clinical trials', *Medicina*, 57(3), pp.199.

246. Doshi, P. (2021) *Pfizer and Moderna's "95% effective" vaccines—we need more details and the raw data.* Available at: https://blogs.bmj.com/bmj/2021/01/04/peter-doshi-pfizer-and-modernas-95-effective-vaccines-we-need-more-details-and-the-raw-data/ (Accessed: 01 08 2021)

247. Del Mar, C. and Collignon, P. (2018) *The flu vaccine is being oversold – it's not that effective.* Available: https://theconversation.com/the-flu-vaccine-is-being-oversold-its-not-that-effective-97688 (Accessed: 20 07 2020)

248. Doshi, P. (2020) 'Will covid-19 vaccines save lives? Current trials aren't designed to tell us', *The British Medical Journal*, 371(m4037).

249. Fortune Business Insights (2020) Influenza Vaccine Market Size, Share & COVID-19 Impact Analysis, By Type (Inactivated and Live Attenuated), By Valency (Quadrivalent and Trivalent), By Age Group (Pediatric and Adults), By Distribution Channel (Hospital & Retail Pharmacies, Government Suppliers and Others) and Geography Forecast, 2020-2027. Available at: https://www.fortunebusinessinsights.com/industry-reports/influenza-vaccine-market-101896 (Accessed: 14 02 2021)

250. US Congress (1986) *H.R.5546 - National Childhood Vaccine Injury Act of 1986.* Available at: https://www.congress.gov/bill/99th-congress/house-bill/5546 (Accessed: 21 02 2020)

251. Sullivan, T (2018) *Supreme Court Rules in Favor of Protecting Vaccine Makers from State Lawsuits.* Available at: https://www.policymed.com/2011/03/supreme-court-rules-in-favor-of-protecting-vaccine-makers-from-state-lawsuits.html (Accessed: 12 11 2020)

252. US Dept. of Health and Human Services (2021) *Public Readiness and Emergency Preparedness Act.* Available at: https://www.phe.gov/Preparedness/legal/prepact/Pages/default.aspx (Accessed: 21 02 2021)

253. HRSA (2021) National Vaccine Injury Compensation Program Data Report (Updated Feb 1 2021)

254. Guarascio, F. (2020) *COVID-19 vaccine makers see EU shield against side-effect claims.* Available at: https://www.reuters.com/article/uk-health-coronavirus-eu-vaccine-idUKKCN26D0UG (Accessed: 21 02 2021)

255. UK Government (2021) Vaccine Damage Payment. Available at: https://www.gov.uk/vaccine-damage-payment (Accessed: 14 02 2021)

256. DWP (2019) *Compensation Paid, Amounts of Unsuccessful & Successful Claims under Vaccine Damage Payment Fund.* Available at: https://www.whatdotheyknow.com/request/574914/response/1368597/attach/html/2/17527 %20Response.pdf.html (Accessed: 15 02 2021)

257. UK.GOV (2020) *Information for Healthcare Professionals on COVID-19 Vaccine AstraZeneca.* Available at: https://www.gov.uk/government/publications/regulatory-approval-of-covid-19-vaccine-astrazeneca/information-for-healthcare-professionals-on-covid-19-vaccine-astrazeneca (Accessed: 02 01 2021)

258. UKDH (2012) *8:Vaccine safety and the management of adverse events following immunisation.* Available at: https://vaccine-safety-training.org/tl_files/vs/pdf/UKDH_GreenBook.pdf (Accessed: 23 08 2021)

259. Wang, F., Kream, R.M. and Stefano, G.B. (2020) 'An evidence based perspective on mRNA-SARS-CoV-2 vaccine development', *Medical science monitor: international medical journal of experimental and clinical research*, 26, pp.1-8.

260. Collignon, P., Doshi, P. and Jefferson, T. (2010) 'Ramifications of adverse events in children in Australia', *The British Medical Journal*, 340(c2994).

261. Schnirring, L. (2014) *CSL studies shed light on 2010 flu vaccine seizures.* Available at: https://www.cidrap.umn.edu/news-perspective/2014/06/csl-studies-shed-light-2010-flu-vaccine-seizures (Accessed: 20 06 2021)

262. Swenson,A (2020) Bill Gates did not say 700,000 people will have negative side effects from a coronavirus vaccine. Available at: https://apnews.com/article/9155890357 (Accessed: 01 11 2020)

263. Moderna (2021) *Clinical Trial Results.* Available at: https://www.modernatx.com/covid19vaccine-eua/providers/clinical-trial-data (Accessed: 21 03 2021)

264. Marshall, M. (2021) *Vaccine side effects are actually a good thing.* Available at: https://www.vox.com/22278795/vaccine-side-effects-moderna-pfizer-covid-19 (Accessed: 02 04 2021)

265. Polyakova, K. (2021) 'Rapid Response: Re: Do doctors have to have the covid-19 vaccine?', *The British Medical Journal*, 372(n810).

266. Novotny, I. (2021) *What are the BMJ's vaccine censors afraid of?* Available at: https://www.conservativewoman.co.uk/what-are-the-bmjs-vaccine-censors-afraid-of/ (Accessed: 16 05 2021)

267. Klein, G., Powers, A. and Croce, C. (2002) 'Association of SV40 with human tumors', *Oncogene*, 21(8), pp.1141-1149.

268. Fisher, S.G., Weber, L. and Carbone, M. (1999) 'Cancer risk associated with simian virus 40 contaminated polio vaccine', *Anticancer research*, 19(3B), pp.2173-2180.

269. Shah, K.V. (2007) 'SV40 and human cancer: a review of recent data', International journal of cancer, 120(2), pp.215-223.

270. Mazzoni, E., Benassi, M.S., Corallini, A., Barbanti-Brodano, G., Taronna, A., Picci, P., Guerra, G., D'Agostino, A., Trevisiol, L., Nocini, P.F. and Casali, M.V. (2015) 'Significant association between human osteosarcoma and simian virus 40', *Cancer*, 121(5), pp.708-715.

271. Mazzoni, E., Pietrobon, S., Bilancia, M., Vinante, F., Rigo, A., Ferrarini, I., D'Agostino, A., Casali, M.V., Martini, F. and Tognon, M. (2017) 'High prevalence of antibodies reacting to mimotopes of Simian virus 40 large T antigen, the oncoprotein, in serum samples of patients affected by non-Hodgkin lymphoma', *Cancer Immunology, Immunotherapy,* 66(9), pp.1189-1198

272. Limam, S., Missaoui, N., Bdioui, A., Yacoubi, M.T., Krifa, H., Mokni, M. and Selmi, B. (2020) 'Investigation of simian virus 40 (SV40) and human JC, BK, MC, KI, and WU polyomaviruses in glioma', *Journal of neurovirology*, 26(3), pp.347-357.

273. Ellis-Petersen, H. (2019) *Pakistan accused of cover-up over fresh polio outbreak.* Available at: https://www.theguardian.com/global-development/2019/nov/07/pakistan-accused-of-cover-up-over-fresh-polio-outbreak (Accessed: 10 11 2020)

274. Akst, J. (2019) *Polio Vaccination Causes More Infections than Wild Virus.* Available at: https://www.the-scientist.com/news-opinion/polio-vaccination-causes-more-infections-than-wild-virus-66778 (Accessed: 13 11 2020)

275. Mohamed, E. (2019) *Polio outbreaks in Africa caused by mutation of strain in vaccine.* Available at: https://www.theguardian.com/global-development/2019/nov/28/polio-outbreaks-in-four-african-countries-caused-by-mutation-of-strain-in-vaccine (Accessed: 13 08 2021)

276. Independent Monitoring Board of the Global Polio Eradication Initiative (2019), *The Art of Survival: The Polio Virus Continues to Exploit Human Frailties.*

277. Dhiman, R., Prakash, S.C., Sreenivas, V. and Puliyel, J. (2018) 'Correlation between Non-Polio Acute Flaccid Paralysis Rates with Pulse Polio Frequency in India', *International Journal of Environmental Research and Public Health*, 15(8), pp.1-7.

278. Offit, P.A. (2005) The cutter incident: How america's first polio vaccine led to a growing vaccine crisis. London: Yale University Press.

279. Davies, M., Furneaux, R., Ruiz, I. and Langlois, J. (2021) *'Held to ransom': Pfizer demands governments gamble with state assets to secure vaccine deal.* Available at: https://www.thebureauinvestigates.com/stories/2021-02-23/held-to-ransom-pfizer-demands-governments-gamble-with-state-assets-to-secure-vaccine-deal (Accessed: 24 02 2021)

280. Sharman, L. (2021) *Double jabbed carry same viral load of Covid as unvaccinated.* Available at: https://www.standard.co.uk/news/uk/double-covid-vaccinated-same-viral-load-unvaccinated-b951377.html (Accessed: 29 08 2021)

281. RT News (2021) 'Nothing else explains it': Norwegian scientists say AstraZeneca DID cause blood clots, as British & Dutch experts dismiss theory. Available at: https://www.rt.com/news/518531-norway-astrazeneca-link-blood-clots/ (Accessed: 31 07 2021)

282. Sterzik, K. (2021) *AstraZeneca: German team discovers thrombosis trigger.* Available at: https://www.dw.com/en/astrazeneca-german-team-discovers-thrombosis-trigger/a-56925550 (Accessed: 24 03 2021)

283. Blanchard, S. and Matthews, S. (2021) Seven British people died from a brain blood clot after AstraZeneca jab out of 18.1MILLION doses - and under-45s are up to 35 TIMES more likely to die of Covid than develop a CSVT. Available at: https://www.dailymail.co.uk/news/article-9429125/UK-regulator-total-30-cases-blood-clot-events-AstraZeneca-vaccine-use.html (Accessed: 07 04 2021)

284. Andrews, L. (2021) European drug regulator chief warns there is now a 'CLEAR' link between AstraZeneca's Covid jab and blood clots - as it is claimed UK WON'T ban vaccine for under-30s amid review over its safety in younger people. Available at: https://www.dailymail.co.uk/news/article-9432593/Expert-suspects-causal-link-AstraZeneca-jab-rare-blood-clots.html (Accessed: 06 04 2021)

285. Doody, K. (2021) *3 people under 30 have died from blood clots after receiving AstraZeneca vaccine.* Available at: https://www.hexham-courant.co.uk/news/national/uk-today/19216220.3-people-30-died-blood-clots-receiving-astrazeneca-vaccine/ (Accessed: 07 04 2021)

286. BBC News (2021) *AstraZeneca vaccine: Denmark stops rollout completely.* Available at: https://www.bbc.co.uk/news/world-europe-56744474 (Accessed: 14 04 2021)

287. Rigby, J. and Nuki, P. (2021) *Revealed: Why Britain's regulator missed the link between the AstraZeneca jab and rare blood clots.* Available at: https://www.telegraph.co.uk/global-health/science-and-disease/revealed-britains-regulator-missed-link-astrazeneca-jab-rare/ (Accessed: 18 04 2021)

288. Dowrick, M. (2021) *Plymouth mum-of-three 'dies with blood clots after AstraZeneca jab'. Available at:* https://www.plymouthherald.co.uk/news/plymouth-news/plymouth-mum-three-dies-blood-5483130 (Accessed: 04 06 2021)

289. Martin, D. and Nicholson, A. (2021) *Mum-of-three dies after receiving AstraZeneca coronavirus vaccine.* Available at: https://www.liverpoolecho.co.uk/news/uk-world-news/mum-three-dies-after-receiving-20915400 (Accessed: 28 06 2021)

290. Sullivan, R. (2021) *BBC presenter died after suffering blood clots following AstraZeneca jab, family says.* Available at: https://www.independent.co.uk/news/health/lisa-shaw-bbc-death-astrazeneca-b1855330.html (Accessed: 28 05 2021)

291. Sinclair, L. (2021) *British model dies days after receiving AstraZeneca vaccine.* Available at: https://www.standard.co.uk/news/uk/british-model-dies-cyprus-astrazeneca-vaccine-b937107.html (Accessed: 29 05 2021)

292. Hope, H. (2001) *'WORRYING' Princess Michael of Kent, 76, ill with blood clots after having two Covid jabs'.* Available at: https://www.thesun.co.uk/news/14968095/princess-michael-of-kent-blood-clots-two-covid-jabs/amp/ (Accessed: 15 05 2021)

293. BBC News (2021) *AstraZeneca vaccine: 'Don't be fobbed off' urges fiancee.* Available at: https://www.bbc.com/news/uk-england-tyne-57677606 (Accessed: 02 07 2021)

294. Lovett, S. (2021) *Woman whose husband died from AstraZeneca vaccine calls for overhaul of outdated compensation scheme.* Available at: https://www.independent.co.uk/independentpremium/covid-vaccine-astrazeneca-uk-side-effects-b1864258.html (Accessed: 14 06 2021)

295. Bodkin, H. (2021) *AstraZeneca working to eliminate risk of blood clots from vaccine.* Available at: https://www.telegraph.co.uk/news/2021/07/13/astrazeneca-working-eliminate-risk-blood-clots-vaccine/ (Accessed: 31 07 2021)

296. Craig, E. (2021) 'Blood on their hands': UK fury at EU leaders for slating AstraZeneca's Covid vaccine 'out of spite over Brexit' after study finds it has the same risk of blood clots as Pfizer's. Available at: https://www.dailymail.co.uk/news/article-9838639/AstraZeneca-vaccine-risk-blood-clots-Pfizers-study-finds.html (Accessed: 30 07 2021)

297. RT News (2021) Viral Twitter post claims 13yo died of 'cardiac event' as doctors consider link between rare heart condition & vaccine in boys. Available at: https://www.rt.com/usa/527177-twitter-vaccine-boy-died-heart/ (Accessed: 24 06 2021)

298. News Rescue (2021) *45 Year Old John Hopkins Hospital Employee Dies After Mandatory Covid Shot This June.* Available at: https://newsrescue.com/45-year-old-john-hopkins-hospital-employee-dies-after-mandatory-covid-shot-this-june/ (Accessed: 15 07 2021)

299. Montgomery, J., Ryan, M., Engler, R., Hoffman, D., McClenathan, B., Collins, L., Loran, D., Hrncir, D., Herring, K., Platzer, M. and Adams, N. (2021) 'Myocarditis following immunization with mRNA COVID-19 vaccines in members of the US military', *JAMA Cardiology*, 2833.

300. Negron, S.G., Kessinger, C.W., Xu, B., Pu, W.T. and Lin, Z. (2021) 'Selectively expressing SARS-CoV-2 Spike protein S1 subunit in cardiomyocytes induces cardiac hypertrophy in mice', *bioRxv* (preprint)

301. Hause, A.M., Gee, J., Baggs, J., Abara, W.E., Marquez, P., Thompson, D., Su, J.R., Licata, C., Rosenblum, H.G., Myers, T.R., Shimabukuro, T.T. and Shay, D.K. (2021) *COVID-19 Vaccine Safety in Adolescents Aged 12–17 Years - United States, December 14, 2020–July 16, 2021.* Available at: https://www.cdc.gov/mmwr/volumes/70/wr/mm7031e1.htm?s_cid=mm7031e1_w (Accessed: 02 08 2021)

302. Grün, S., Schumm, J., Greulich, S., Wagner, A., Schneider, S., Bruder, O., Kispert, E.M., Hill, S., Ong, P., Klingel, K. and Kandolf, R. (2012) 'Long-term follow-up of biopsy-proven viral myocarditis: predictors of mortality and incomplete recovery', *Journal of the American College of Cardiology*, 5(18), pp.1604-1615.

303. Melbourne Vaccine Education Centre (2021) *Thrombosis with thrombocytopenia syndrome (TTS).* Available at: https://mvec.mcri.edu.au/references/thrombosis-with-thrombocytopenia-syndrome/ (Accessed: 14 07 2021)

304. Wolins, N., Lozier, J., Eggerman, T.L., Jones, E., Aguilar-Cordova, E. and Vostal, J.G. (2003) 'Intravenous administration of replication-incompetent adenovirus to rhesus monkeys induces thrombocytopenia by increasing in vivo platelet clearance', *British Journal of Haematology*, 123(5), pp.903-905.

305. Othman, M., Labelle, A., Mazzetti, I., Elbatarny, H.S. and Lillicrap, D. (2007) 'Adenovirus-induced thrombocytopenia: the role of von Willebrand factor and P-selectin in mediating accelerated platelet clearance', *Blood*, 109(7), pp.2832-2839.

306. Kowarz, E., Krutzke, L., Reis, J., Bracharz, S., Kochanek, S. and Marschalek, R. (2021) '"Vaccine-Induced Covid-19 Mimicry" Syndrome: Splice reactions within the SARS-CoV-2 Spike open reading frame result in Spike protein variants that may cause thromboembolic events in patients immunized with vector-based vaccines.', *Research Square*, pp.1-17.

307. Beeler, J., Varricchio, F. and Wise, R. (1996) 'Thrombocytopenia after immunization with measles vaccines: review of the vaccine adverse events reporting system (1990 to 1994)', *The Pediatric infectious disease journal*, 15(1), pp.88-90.

308. Stuijver, D.J., Romualdi, E., van Zaane, B., Bax, L., Büller, H.R., Gerdes, V.E. and Squizzato, A. (2015) 'Under-reporting of venous and arterial thrombotic events in randomized clinical trials: a meta-analysis', Internal and emergency medicine, 10(2), pp.219-246.

309. Syal, A. (2021) *Covid vaccines may not protect people with immune disorders. NIH trial seeks answers.* Available at: https://www.nbcnews.com/health/health-news/covid-vaccines-may-not-protect-people-immune-disorders-nih-trial-n1266886 (Accessed: 06 06 2021)

310. Jones, W. (2021) *Why Are People Unwell with Symptomatic COVID-19 Being Vaccinated?* Available at: https://lockdownsceptics.org/2021/05/23/why-are-people-unwell-with-symptomatic-covid-19-being-vaccinated/ (Accessed: 23 05 2021)

311. Reuters (2021) *Cambodia begins Covid-19 vaccinations with shots for PM's sons, ministers.* Available at: https://www.bangkokpost.com/world/2065891/cambodia-begins-covid-19-vaccinations-with-shots-for-pms-sons-ministers (Accessed: 11 02 2021)

312. Al Jazeera (2021) *Cambodia reports first COVID death amid new outbreak.* Available at: https://www.aljazeera.com/news/2021/3/11/cambodia-reports-first-covid-death-amid-new-outbreak (Accessed: 12 03 2021)

313. Cork, T. (2021) *Inside the care home in Bristol where residents were vaccinated 'well before' Covid-19 outbreak.* Bristol Live. Available at: https://www.bristolpost.co.uk/news/bristol-news/inside-care-home-bristol-residents-4965298 (Accessed: 07 02 2021)

314. Deutsche Welle (2021) *Coronavirus digest: German nursing home sees outbreak after vaccines.* Available at: https://www.dw.com/en/coronavirus-digest-german-nursing-home-sees-outbreak-after-vaccines/a-56491823 (Accessed: 09 02 2021)

315. Torjesen, I. (2021) 'Covid-19: Norway investigates 23 deaths in frail elderly patients after vaccination', *The British Medical Journal,* 372(n149).

316. Uguen-Csenge, E. (2021) *New outbreak of COVID-19 in B.C. care home where 82% of residents were already vaccinated.* Available at: https://www.cbc.ca/news/canada/british-columbia/new-outbreak-covid-bc-care-home-1.5941508 (Accessed: 23 03 2021)

317. Egan,C., Knight, S.,Baillie, K., Harrison, E., Docherty, A. and Semple, C. (2021) *Hospitalised vaccinated patients during the second wave, update April '21.* ISARIC4C / CO-CIN

318. Binding, L. (2021) COVID-19: Staff at mass vaccination centre in Cardiff test positive for coronavirus. Available at: https://news.sky.com/story/covid-19-staff-at-mass-vaccination-centre-in-cardiff-test-positive-for-coronavirus-12163535 (Accessed: 17 12 2021)

319. Smatti, M.K., Al Thani, A.A. and Yassine, H.M. (2018) 'Viral-induced enhanced disease illness', *Frontiers in microbiology*, 9, pp.2991.

320. Iwasaki, A., Yang, Y. (2020) 'The potential danger of suboptimal antibody responses in COVID-19', *Nature Reviews | Immunology*, 20(6), pp.339-341.

321. Arvin, A.M., Fink, K., Schmid, M.A., Cathcart, A., Spreafico, R., Havenar-Daughton, C., Lanzavecchia, A., Corti, D. and Virgin, H.W. (2020) 'A perspective on potential antibody-dependent enhancement of SARS-CoV-2', Nature, 584(7821), pp.353-363.

322. Peron, J.P.S. and Nakaya, H. (2020) 'Susceptibility of the Elderly to SARS-CoV-2 Infection: ACE-2 Overexpression, Shedding, and Antibodydependent Enhancement (ADE)', *Clinics*, 75(e1912), pp.1-6

323. Forni, G. and Mantovani, A. (2021) 'COVID-19 vaccines: where we stand and challenges ahead', *Cell Death & Differentiation*, 28(2), pp.626-639.

324. Lee, W.S., Wheatley, A.K., Kent, S.J. and DeKosky, B.J. (2020) 'Antibody-dependent enhancement andSARS-CoV-2 vaccines and therapies', *Nature microbiology*, 5(10), pp.1185-1191.

325. Cardozo, T. and Veazey, R. (2021) 'Informed consent disclosure to vaccine trial subjects of risk of COVID-19 vaccines worsening clinical disease', *International journal of clinical practice*, 75(3), p.e13795

326. Yu, J., Tostanoski, L.H., Peter, L., Mercado, N.B., McMahan, K., Mahrokhian, S.H., Nkolola, J.P., Liu, J., Li, Z., Chandrashekar, A. and Martinez, D.R. (2020) 'DNA vaccine protection against SARS-CoV-2 in rhesus macaques', *Science*, 369(6505), pp.806-811.

327. Corbett, K.S., Flynn, B., Foulds, K.E., Francica, J.R., Boyoglu-Barnum, S., Werner, A.P., Flach, B., O'Connell, S., Bock, K.W., Minai, M. and Nagata, B.M. (2020) 'Evaluation of the mRNA-1273 vaccine against SARS-CoV-2 in nonhuman primates', *New England Journal of Medicine*, 383(16), pp.1544-1555.

328. ZOE Study (2021) *Vaccine after effects more common in those who already had COVID.* Available at: https://covid.joinzoe.com/post/vaccine-after-effects-more-common-in-those-who-already-had-covid (Accessed: 14 05 2021)

329. Lyons-Weiler, J. (2020) 'Pathogenic priming likely contributes to serious and critical illness and mortality in COVID-19 via autoimmunity', *Journal of translational autoimmunity*, 3(100051), pp.1-5

330. Segal, Y. and Shoenfeld, Y. (2018) 'Vaccine-induced autoimmunity: the role of molecular mimicry and immune crossreaction', *Cellular & molecular immunology,* 15(6), pp.586-594.

331. Eschner, K. (2017) *The Long Shadow of the 1976 Swine Flu Vaccine 'Fiasco'.* Available at: https://www.smithsonianmag.com/smart-news/long-shadow-1976-swine-flu-vaccine-fiasco-180961994/ (Accessed: 12 09 2020)

332. Leslie, D.L., Kobre, R.A., Richmand, B.J., Aktan Guloksuz, S. and Leckman, J.F. (2017) 'Temporal Association of Certain Neuropsychiatric Disorders Following Vaccination of Children and Adolescents: A Pilot Case–Control Study', Frontiers in Psychiatry, 8, pp.1-8.

333. Wang, K. (2017) *Vaccines linked to mental disorders by Yale study.* Available at: https://yaledailynews.com/blog/2017/02/21/vaccines-linked-to-mental-disorders-by-yale-study/ (Accessed: 24 06 2021)

334. Rhea, E.M., Logsdon, A.F., Hansen, K.M., Williams, L.M., Reed, M.J., Baumann, K.K., Holden, S.J., Raber, J., Banks, W.A. and Erickson, M.A. (2020) 'The S1 protein of SARS-CoV-2 crosses the blood–brain barrier in mice', *Nature Neuroscience*, 24(3), pp.368-378.

174

335. Buzhdygan, T.P., DeOre, B.J., Baldwin-Leclair, A., Bullock, T.A., McGary, H.M., Khan, J.A., Razmpour, R., Hale, J.F., Galie, P.A., Potula, R. and Andrews, A.M. (2021) 'The SARS-CoV-2 spike protein alters barrier function in 2D static and 3D microfluidic in-vitro models of the human blood–brain barrier', *Neurobiology of Disease*, 146 (105131), pp. 1-12.

336. Desforges, M., Le Coupanec, A., Dubeau, P., Bourgouin, A., Lajoie, L., Dubé, M. and Talbot, P.J. (2020) 'Human coronaviruses and other respiratory viruses: underestimated opportunistic pathogens of the central nervous system?', *Viruses*, 12(1), pp.1-28.

337. Tseng, C.T., Sbrana, E., Iwata-Yoshikawa, N., Newman, P.C., Garron, T., Atmar, R.L., Peters, C.J. and Couch, R.B. (2012) 'Immunization with SARS coronavirus vaccines leads to pulmonary immunopathology on challenge with the SARS virus.' *PloS one*, 7(4), p.e35421.

338. Zhang, L., Richards, A., Barrasa, M.I., Hughes, S.H., Young, R.A. and Jaenisch, R. (2021) 'Reverse-transcribed SARS-CoV-2 RNA can integrate into the genome of cultured human cells and can be expressed in patient-derived tissues', PNAS, 118(21), pp.1-10.

339. de Vrieze, J. (2020) *Suspicions grow that nanoparticles in Pfizer's COVID-19 vaccine trigger rare allergic reactions.* Available at: https://www.sciencemag.org/news/2020/12/suspicions-grow-nanoparticles-pfizer-s-covid-19-vaccine-trigger-rare-allergic-reactions (Accessed: 21 12 2020)

340. Wylon, K., Dölle, S. and Worm, M. (2016) 'Polyethylene glycol as a cause of anaphylaxis', *Allergy, Asthma & Clinical Immunology*, 12(1), pp.1-3.

341. Yang, Q., Jacobs, T.M., McCallen, J.D., Moore, D.T., Huckaby, J.T., Edelstein, J.N. and Lai, S.K. (2016) 'Analysis of pre-existing IgG and IgM antibodies against polyethylene glycol (PEG) in the general population', *Analytical chemistry*, 88(23), pp.11804-11812.

342. Zhu, Y.T., Yuan, Y.Z., Feng, Q.P., Hu, M.Y., Li, W.J., Wu, X., Xiang, S.Y. and Yu, S.Q. (2021) 'Food emulsifier polysorbate 80 promotes the intestinal absorption of mono-2-ethylhexyl phthalate by disturbing intestinal barrier', *Toxicology and Applied Pharmacology*, 414, pp.1-14.

343. Olivier, J.C., Fenart, L., Chauvet, R., Pariat, C., Cecchelli, R. and Couet, W. (1999) 'Indirect evidence that drug brain targeting using polysorbate 80-coated polybutylcyanoacrylate nanoparticles is related to toxicity.' *Pharmaceutical research*, 16(12), pp.1836-1842.

344. Badiu, I., Geuna, M., Heffler, E. and Rolla, G. (2012) 'Hypersensitivity reaction to human papillomavirus vaccine due to polysorbate 80', *BMJ Case Reports*, 10.1136/bcr.02.2012.5797

345. National Toxicology Program, 1992. NTP toxicology and carcinogenesis studies of polysorbate 80 (CAS no. 9005-65-6) in F344/N rats and B6C3F1 mice (feed studies). *National Toxicology Program technical report series*, 415, pp.1-225.

346. Tatsuishi, T., Oyama, Y., Iwase, K., Yamaguchi, J.Y., Kobayashi, M., Nishimura, Y., Kanada, A. and Hirama, S. (2005) 'Polysorbate 80 increases the susceptibility to oxidative stress in rat thymocytes', *Toxicology*, 207(1), pp.7-14.

347. Hatziantoniou, S., Maltezou, H.C., Tsakris, A., Poland, G.A. and Anastassopoulou, C. (2021) 'Anaphylactic reactions to mRNA COVID-19 vaccines: A call for further study', *Vaccine*, 39(19), pp.2605–2607.

348. Hernández, A.F., Calina, D., Poulas, K., Docea, A.O. and Tsatsakis, A.M. (2021) 'Safety of COVID-19 vaccines administered in the EU: Should we be concerned?', Toxicology Reports, 8, pp.871-879.

349. Talotta, R. and Robertson, E.S. (2021) 'Antiphospholipid antibodies and risk of post-COVID-19 vaccination thrombophilia: The straw that breaks the camel's back?', *Cytokine & Growth Factor Reviews*, 60, pp.52-60.

350. Kennedy, D.A. and Read, A.F. (2017) 'Why does drug resistance readily evolve but vaccine resistance does not?', *Proceedings of the Royal Society B: Biological Sciences*, 284(1851), pp.1-9.

351. Wang, B., Shao, X., Wang, D., Xu, D. and Zhang, J.A. (2017) 'Vaccinations and risk of systemic lupus erythematosus and rheumatoid arthritis: A systematic review and meta-analysis', *Autoimmunity Reviews*, 16(7), pp.756-765.

352. Public Health England (2021) What to expect after your COVID-19 vaccination. Available at: https://www.gov.uk/government/publications/covid-19-vaccination-what-to-expect-after-vaccination/what-to-expect-after-your-covid-19-vaccination (Accessed: 01 02 2021)

353. Vaughan, A. (2021) *UK advisers cautious about how much covid-19 vaccines cut transmission.* Available at: https://www.newscientist.com/article/2266150-uk-advisers-cautious-about-how-much-covid-19-vaccines-cut-transmission/ (Accessed: 01 02 2021)

354. Scientific Advisory Group for Emergencies (2021) *S1335 Long term evolution of SARS-CoV-2: Can we predict the limits of SARS-CoV-2 variants and their phenotypic consequences?* Available at: https://assets.publishing.service.gov.uk/government/uploads/system/uploads/attachment_data/file/1007566/S1335_Long_term_evolution_of_SARS-CoV-2.pdf (Accessed: 24 08 2021)

355. RT News (2021) UK government panel claims Covid mutation with 35% death rate a 'realistic possibility,' suggests new strains may 'evade' vaccines. Available at: https://www.rt.com/uk/530756-covid-mutations-death-rate/ (Accessed: 31 07 2021)

356. Read, A.F., Baigent, S.J., Powers, C., Kgosana, L.B., Blackwell, L., Smith, L.P., Kennedy, D.A., Walkden-Brown, S.W. and Nair. V.K. (2015) 'Imperfect vaccination can enhance the transmission of highly virulent pathogens', *PLoS Biology*, 13(7), p.e1002198.

357. Nal, R. (2021) *Bombshell: Nobel Prize Winner Reveals - Covid Vaccine is 'Creating Variants'.* Available at: https://rairfoundation.com/bombshell-nobel-prize-winner-reveals-covid-vaccine-is-creating-variants/ (Accessed: 21 05 2021)

358. Lauring, A.S. and Hodcroft, E.B. (2021) 'Genetic variants of SARS-CoV-2—what do they mean?' *Jama*, 325(6), pp.529-531.

359. Skribent, E. (2021) *Geert Vanden Bossche: "We must halt all ongoing Covid-19 mass vaccination campaigns".* Available at: https://newsvoice.se/2021/03/geert-vanden-bossche-halt-covid-19-mass-vaccination/ (Accessed: 24 08 2021)

360. Garcia-Beltran, W.F., Lam, E.C., Denis, K.S., Nitido, A.D., Garcia, Z.H., Hauser, B.M., Feldman, J., Pavlovic, M.N., Gregory, D.J., Poznansky, M.C. and Sigal, A., 2021. 'Multiple SARS-CoV-2 variants escape neutralization by vaccine-induced humoral immunity.' *Cell*, 184(9), pp.2372-2383.

361. Planas, D., Veyer, D., Baidaliuk, A., Staropoli, I., Guivel-Benhassine, F., Rajah, M.M., Planchais, C., Porrot, F., Robillard, N., Puech, J. and Prot, M. (2021) 'Reduced sensitivity of SARS-CoV-2 variant Delta to antibody neutralization', Nature, 596, pp.1-8.

362. Sample, I., Geddes, L. (2021) *Covid vaccines may need updating to protect against new variant, study suggests.* Available at: https://www.theguardian.com/society/2021/jan/20/covid-vaccines-may-need-updating-to-protect-against-new-variant-study-suggests (Accessed: 21 01 2021)

363. Black, R. (2021) *Annual or bi-annual Covid-19 vaccination may be required.* Available at: https://www.irishnews.com/news/healthcarenews/2021/01/12/news/-annual-or-bi-annual-covid-19-vaccination-may-be-required--2185096/ (Accessed: 24 08 2021)

364. Brawer, A.E. and Sullivan, D. H. (2020) 'The expanding cocktail of harmful ingredients in human papillomavirus vaccines', *Frontiers in Women's Health*, 5, pp.1-4.

365. LaFraniere, S. and Weiland, N. (2021) *F.D.A. Releases More of Johnson & Johnson's Vaccine, but Baltimore Plant Remains Closed.* Available at: https://www.nytimes.com/2021/07/02/us/politics/johnson-johnson-vaccine-batch.html (Accessed: 09 07 2021)

366. Idrees, D. and Kumar, V. (2021) 'SARS-CoV-2 spike protein interactions with amyloidogenic proteins: Potential clues to neurodegeneration', *Biochemical and Biophysical Research Communications*, 554, pp.94-98.

367. Song, E., Zhang, C., Israelow, B., Lu-Culligan, A., Prado, A.V., Skriabine, S., Lu, P., Weizman, O.E., Liu, F., Dai, Y. and Szigeti-Buck, K. (2021) 'Neuroinvasion of SARS-CoV-2 in human and mouse brain', *Journal of Experimental Medicine*, 218(3), p.e20202135.

368. Lamontagne, N. (2021) *SARS-CoV-2 spike protein alone may cause lung damage.* Available at: https://eurekalert.org/pub_releases/2021-04/eb-ssp041621.php (Accessed: 02 06 2021)

369. Lamontagne, N. (2021) *Gene changes might explain long-haul COVID-19 symptoms.* Available at: https://www.eurekalert.org/pub_releases/2021-04/eb-gcm041621.php (Accessed: 02 06 2021)

370. Suzuki, Y.J. and Gychka, S.G. (2021) 'Spike Protein Elicits Cell Signaling in Human Host Cells: Implications for Possible Consequences of COVID-19 Vaccines', *Vaccines*, 9(1), pp.1-8.

371. Pierson, A. (2021) *New peer reviewed study on COVID-19 vaccines suggests why heart inflammation, blood clots and other*. Available at: https://omny.fm/shows/on-point-with-alex-pierson/new-peer-reviewed-study-on-covid-19-vaccines-sugge/ (Accessed: 29 05 2021)

372. Classen, J.B. (2021) 'COVID-19 RNA Based Vaccines and the Risk of Prion Disease', *Microbiol Infect Dis*, 5(1), pp.1-3.

373. Young, M.J., O'Hare, M., Matiello, M. and Schmahmann, J.D. (2020) 'Creutzfeldt-Jakob disease in a man with COVID-19: SARS-CoV-2-accelerated neurodegeneration?', *Brain, behavior, and immunity*, 89, pp.601-603.

374. Public Health England (2012) *8:Vaccine safety and the management of adverse events following immunisation.* Available at: https://assets.publishing.service.gov.uk/government/uploads/system/uploads/attachment_data/file/147868/Green-Book-Chapter-8-v4_0.pdf (Accessed: 08 06 2020)

375. RT News (2021) Cold chain strikes again: 1,900 doses of Moderna vaccine go poof in Boston after cleaner reportedly unplugged freezer. Available at: https://www.rt.com/usa/513306-vaccine-wasted-pulled-plug/ (Accessed: 23 01 2021)

376. ABC 7 Chicago (2020) *Nearly 500 Moderna COVID vaccine doses discarded in Grafton, Wisconsin.* Available at: https://abc7chicago.com/wisconsin-grafton-wi-moderna-vaccine-covid/9169782/ (Accessed: 24 08 2021)

377. RT News (2020) Employee fired for 'INTENTIONALLY' removing dozens of Covid-19 vaccine vials from freezer, FBI & police investigating. Available at: https://www.rt.com/usa/511186-moderna-vaccines-fbi-case/ (Accessed: 01 01 2021)

378. RT News (2021) *Swedish health agency investigates after 1,000 people receive Moderna vaccine kept at too low a temperature.* Available at: https://www.rt.com/news/513358-sweden-moderna-too-cold/ (Accessed: 22 01 2021)

379. Salo, J. (2021) *Walgreens store mistakenly injects saline instead of COVID-19 vaccine.*
Available at: https://nypost.com/2021/04/19/walgreens-store-injected-saline-instead-of-
covid-19-vaccine/ (Accessed: 12 07 2021)

380. Impelli, M. (2021) *Group of Canadians Accidentally Receive Saline Injection Instead of
COVID-19 Vaccine.* Available at: https://www.newsweek.com/group-canadians-accidentally-
receive-saline-injection-instead-covid-19-vaccine-1585544 (Accessed: 12 07 2021)

381. Godfrey, C. (2021) *Patients receive saline shots instead of COVID-19 vaccine doses in
Sauk Centre.* Available at: https://www.fox9.com/news/2-patients-receive-saline-shots-
instead-of-covid-19-vaccine-doses-in-sauk-centre (Accessed: 12 07 2021)

382. Kato, Y. (2021) *Japanese hospital mistakenly gives saline solution shot instead of COVID-
19 vaccine.* Available at: https://mainichi.jp/english/articles/20210513/p2a/00m/0na/004000c
(Accessed: 12 07 2021)

383. RT News (2021) *Quebec officials launch probe after 97yo with dementia given both Pzer &
Moderna Covid jabs, violating guidance.* Available at: https://www.rt.com/news/513472-
quebec-moderna-pfizer-accident-vaccine-dose/ (Accessed: 02 02 2021)

384. ABC News (2021) *COVID-19 Pfizer vaccine incorrectly administered to two patients at
Brisbane aged care home.* Available at: https://www.abc.net.au/news/2021-02-
24/coronavirus-queensland-covid-vaccine-rollout-aged-care-brisbane/13179280 (Accessed:
24 02 2021)

385. Choy, G. and Cheung, E. (2021) *Hong Kong coronavirus: cancer patient given wrong
vaccine after mixing up inoculation centres.* Available at:
https://www.scmp.com/coronavirus/health-medicine/article/3128228/wrong-coronavirus-
vaccine-given-hong-kong-cancer (Accessed: 04 04 2021)

386. Campanile, C. (2021) *Defective COVID shots given at Times Square vaccination site.* Available at: https://www.foxnews.com/us/defective-covid-shots-given-at-times-square-vaccination-site (Accessed: 17 06 2021)

387. CBC News (2021) *Vancouver teenager was one of 12 mistakenly given Moderna instead of Pfizer vaccine.* Available at: https://www.cbc.ca/news/canada/british-columbia/vancouver-teens-given-wrong-covid19-vaccine-1.6046473 (Accessed: 12 06 2021)

388. Vincent, P. and Parsons, L. (2021) Health bosses admit HUGE blunder which saw 163 students at an elite private school given the coveted Pfizer jab despite highly sought-after vaccine only being available to over-40s. Available at: https://www.nytimes.com/2020/07/16/health/coronavirus-vaccine-novavax.html (Accessed: 09 07 2021)

389. Tinari, S. (2021) 'The EMA covid-19 data leak, and what it tells us about mRNA instability.' *The British Medical Journal*, 8283(n627).

390. Mishra, M. (2021) *J&J COVID-19 vaccine manufacturing halted at U.S. plant that had contamination issue.* Available at: https://www.reuters.com/business/healthcare-pharmaceuticals/fda-tells-emergent-plant-behind-botched-covid-19-vaccines-stop-manufacturing-2021-04-19/ (Accessed: 29 05 2021)

391. Krutzke, L., Rösler, R., Wiese, S. and Kochanek, S. (2021) 'Process-related impurities in the ChAdOx1 nCov-19 vaccine', Research Square (Preprint).

392. Agence France-Presse (2021) *Interpol warns fake vaccines seized in China and South Africa are 'tip of iceberg'.* Available at: https://www.theguardian.com/world/2021/mar/04/interpol-warns-fake-vaccines-seized-in-china-and-south-africa-are-tip-of-iceberg (Accessed: 08 03 2021)

393. Averre, D. (2021) *Doctors are arrested for fake Covid vaccine scam where 2,500 people were injected with SEA WATER in India.* Available at: https://www.dailymail.co.uk/news/article-9760011/Doctors-arrested-Covid-vaccine-scam-injecting-2500-people-SEA-WATER-India.html (Accessed: 12 07 2021)

394. Corera, G. (2020) *Coronavirus: Hackers targeted Covid vaccine supply 'cold chain'.* Available at: https://www.bbc.co.uk/news/technology-55165552 (Accessed: 03 12 2020)

395. Puzis, R.,Farbiash, D., Brodt, O.,Elovici, Y. and Greenbaum, D. (2020) 'Increased cyber-biosecurity for DNA synthesis', *Nature Biotechnology*, 38, pp.1379-1381.

396. Medical and Healthcare Products Regulatory Agency (2021) *Coronavirus (COVID-19) vaccine adverse reactions.* Available at: https://www.gov.uk/government/publications/coronavirus-covid-19-vaccine-adverse-reactions (Accessed: 04 08 2021)

397. Ugalmugle, S. and Swain, R. (2020) *Vaccine Market worth over $81.5bn by 2026.* Available at: https://www.gminsights.com/pressrelease/vaccines-market (Accessed: 18 02 2021)

398. Hegazi, A. (2020) 'Market Analysis of 3rd International Conference on Vaccine & Vaccination', *J Immunol Tech Infect Dis*, 8(2).

399. RT News (2021) *Obscene to put profits before saving lives: 9 new Big Pharma billionaires emerge amid Covid-19 vaccine roll out.* Available at: https://www.rt.com/news/524294-vaccine-billionaires-patent-waiver/ (Accessed: 20 05 2021)

400. Vincent, M.J., Bergeron, E., Benjannet, S., Erickson, B.R., Rollin, P.E., Ksiazek, T.G., Seidah, N.G. and Nichol, S.T. (2005) 'Chloroquine is a potent inhibitor of SARS coronavirus infection and spread', *Virology journal*, 2(1), pp.1-10.

401. Mehra, M.R., Ruschitza, F. and Patel, A.N. (2020) 'Retraction—Hydroxychloroquine or chloroquine with or without a macrolide for treatment of COVID-19: a multinational registry analysis', *The Lancet*, 395(10240), p.1820.

402. World Tribune (2020) *Doctor fired, web site taken down after viral video on hydroxychloroquine.* Available at: https://www.worldtribune.com/doctor-fired-web-site-taken-down-after-viral-video-on-hydroxychloroquine/ (Accessed: 17 05 2021)

403. Mercola, J. (2021) *Dr. Vladimir Zelenko Was Profoundly Persecuted for Speaking the Covid Truth.* Available at: https://stateofthenation.co/?p=51722 (Accessed: 02 03 2021)

404. Chen, Y., Li, M.X., Lu, G.D., Shen, H.M. and Zhou, J. (2021) 'Hydroxychloroquine/Chloroquine as Therapeutics for COVID-19: Truth under the Mystery', *International Journal of Biological Sciences*, 17(6), pp.1538-1546.

405. Mittal, N., Mittal, R., Gupta, M.C., Kaushal, J., Chugh, A., Khera, D. and Singh, S. (2021) 'Systematic review and meta-analysis of efficacy and safety of hydroxychloroquine and chloroquine in the treatment of COVID-19', *Journal of Family Medicine and Primary Care*, 10(6), pp.2126-2139.

406. National Institute for Health and Care Excellence (2014) *Vitamin D: supplement use in specific population groups.* Available at: https://www.nice.org.uk/guidance/ph56/chapter/about-this-guideline (Accessed: 24 08 2021)

407. Scipioni, J. (2020) *The supplement Dr. Fauci takes to help keep his immune system healthy.* Available at: https://www.cnbc.com/2020/09/14/supplements-white-house-advisor-fauci-takes-every-day-to-help-keep-his-immune-system-healthy.html (Accessed: 05 08 2021)

408. Dror, A.A., Morozov, N., Daoud, A., Namir, Y., Orly, Y., Shachar, Y., Lifshitz, M., Segal, E., Fischer, L., Mizrachi, M. and Eisenbach, N. (2021) 'Pre-infection 25-hydroxyvitamin D3 levels and association with severity of COVID-19 illness', *medRxiv (Preprint)*

409. Teshome, A., Adane, A., Girma, B. and Mekonnen, Z.A. (2021) 'The impact of vitamin D level on COVID-19 infection: systematic review and meta-analysis', *Frontiers in Public Health*, 9, pp.1-10.

410. Shah, K., Pandya, A. and Saxena, D. (2021) 'Low vitamin D levels and prognosis in a COVID-19 paediatric population: a systematic review', *QJM: An International Journal of Medicine (Preprint)*

411. Pal, R., Banerjee, M., Bhadada, S.K., Shetty, A.J., Singh, B. and Vyas, A. (2021) 'Vitamin D supplementation and clinical outcomes in COVID-19: a systematic review and meta-analysis', *Journal of endocrinological investigation*, pp.1-16.

412. Hariyanto, T.I., Intan, D., Hananto, J.E., Harapan, H. and Kurniawan, A. (2021) 'Vitamin D supplementation and Covid-19 outcomes: A systematic review, meta-analysis and meta-regression', *Reviews in Medical Virology (Preprint)*, pp.1-13.

413. Liel, Y., Ulmer, E., Shary, J., Hollis, B.W. and Bell, N.H. (1988) 'Low Circulating Vitamin D in Obesity', *Calcified tissue international*, 43(4), pp.199-201.

414. Wortsman, J., Matsuoka, L.Y., Chen, T.C., Lu, Z. and Holick, M.F. (2000) 'Decreased bioavailability of vitamin D in obesity', *American journal of clinical nutrition*, 72(3), pp.690-693.

415. Yang, J., Hu, J. and Zhu, C. (2021) 'Obesity aggravates COVID-19: A systematic review and meta-analysis', Medical virology, 93(1), pp.257-261.

416. Kumssa, D.B., Joy, E.J., Ander, E.L., Watts, M.J., Young, S.D., Walker, S. and Broadley, M.R. (2015) 'Dietary calcium and zinc deficiency risks are decreasing but remain prevalent', Scientific reports, 5(10974), pp.1-11.

417. Our World in Data (2021) *Number of Deaths Per Year: World.* Available at: https://ourworldindata.org/grapher/number-of-deaths-per-year?country=~OWID_WRL (Accessed: 08 08 2021)

418. Carlucci, P.M., Ahuja, T., Petrilli, C., Rajagopalan, H., Jones, S. and Rahimian, J. (2020) 'Zinc sulfate in combination with a zinc ionophore may improve outcomes in hospitalized COVID-19 patients', *Journal of medical microbiology*, 69(10), pp.1228-1234.

419. Derwand, R., Scholz, M. and Zelenko, V. (2020) 'COVID-19 outpatients: early risk-stratified treatment with zinc plus low-dose hydroxychloroquine and azithromycin: a retrospective case series study', *International journal of antimicrobial agents*, 56(6), pp.1-10.

420. European Society of Clinical Microbiology and Infectious Diseases (2020) *Lower zinc levels in the blood are associated with an increased risk of death in patients with COVID-19.* Available at: https://medicalxpress.com/news/2020-09-zinc-blood-death-patients-covid-.html (Accessed: 08 08 2021)

421. Te Velthuis, A.J., van den Worm, S.H., Sims, A.C., Baric, R.S., Snijder, E.J. and van Hemert, M.J. (2010) 'Zn2+ Inhibits Coronavirus and Arterivirus RNA Polymerase Activity In Vitro and Zinc Ionophores Block the Replication of These Viruses in Cell Culture', *PLoS pathogens*, 6(11), p.e1001176.

422. Kory, P., Meduri, G.U., Varon, J., Iglesias, J. and Marik, P.E. (2021) 'Review of the Emerging Evidence Demonstrating the Efficacy of Ivermectin in the Prophylaxis and Treatment of COVID-19', *American Journal of Therapeutics*, 28(3), pp.e299–e318.

423. Bryant, A., Lawrie, T.A., Dowswell, T., Fordham, E.J., Scott, M., Hill, S.R. and Tham, T.C.
(2021) 'Ivermectin for Prevention and Treatment of COVID-19 Infection: A Systematic
Review, Meta-analysis, and Trial Sequential Analysis to Inform Clinical Guidelines',
American Journal of Therapeutics, 28(4), pp.e434-e460.

424. Hill, A., Abdulamir, A., Ahmed, S., Asghar, A., Babalola, O.E., Basri, R., Chaccour, C.,
Chachar, A.Z.K., Chowdhury, A.T.M., Elgazzar, A. and Ellis, L. (2021) 'Meta-analysis of
randomized trials of ivermectin to treat SARS-CoV-2 infection', *Open Forum Infectious
Diseases*, Ofab358, pp.1-50

425. Fordham, E. (2021) *Scandal of the suppressed case for ivermectin.* Available at:
https://www.conservativewoman.co.uk/scandal-of-the-suppressed-case-for-ivermectin/
(Accessed: 07 08 2021)

426. Front Line COVID-19 Critical Care Alliance (2021) *Prevention and Treatment Protocols for
COVID-19.* Available at: https://covid19criticalcare.com/covid-19-protocols/ (Accessed: 08
08 2021)

427. Husebo, W. (2021) *Dr. Anthony Fauci One Year Ago: 'People Should Not Be Walking
Around with Masks'.* Available at: https://www.breitbart.com/politics/2021/03/08/dr-anthony-
fauci-one-year-ago-people-should-not-be-walking-around-with-masks/ (Accessed: 08 08
2021)

428. Xiao, J., Shiu, E.Y., Gao, H., Wong, J.Y., Fong, M.W., Ryu, S. and Cowling, B.J. (2020)
'Nonpharmaceutical measures for pandemic influenza in nonhealthcare settings—personal
protective and environmental measures', *Emerging infectious diseases*, 26(5), pp.967-975.

429. Orr, N.W. (1981) 'Is a mask necessary in the operating theatre?', Annals of the Royal
College of Surgeons of England, 63(6), pp.390-392.

430. John Hardie, B.D.S. (2016) 'Why Face Masks Don't Work: A Revealing Review.' *Oral
Health,* pp.64-72.

431. Bundgaard, H., Bundgaard, J.S., Raaschou-Pedersen, D.E.T., von Buchwald, C., Todsen, T., Norsk, J.B., Pries-Heje, M.M., Vissing, C.R., Nielsen, P.B., Winsløw, U.C. and Fogh, K. (2021) 'Effectiveness of adding a mask recommendation to other public health measures to prevent SARS-CoV-2 infection in Danish mask wearers: a randomized controlled trial.' *Annals of Internal Medicine*, 174(3), pp.335-343.

432. MacIntyre, C.R., Seale, H., Dung, T.C., Hien, N.T., Nga, P.T., Chughtai, A.A., Rahman, B., Dwyer, D.E. and Wang, Q. (2015) 'A cluster randomised trial of cloth masks compared with medical masks in healthcare workers', *BMJ open*, 5(4), pp.1-10.

433. Rancourt, D.G. (2020) *Masks Don't Work: A review of science relevant to COVID-19 social policy.* Available at: https://covidinfos.net/wp-content/uploads/2020/05/MasksDon-twork-4.pdf (Accessed: 15 July 2020)

434. Bałazy, A., Toivola, M., Adhikari, A., Sivasubramani, S.K., Reponen, T. and Grinshpun, S.A. (2006) 'Do N95 respirators provide 95% protection level against airborne viruses, and how adequate are surgical masks?' *American journal of infection control*, 34(2), pp.51-57.

435. Davies, A., Thompson, K.A., Giri, K., Kafatos, G., Walker, J. and Bennett, A. (2013) 'Testing the efficacy of homemade masks: would they protect in an influenza pandemic?' *Disaster medicine and public health preparedness*, 7(4), pp.413-418.

436. Lai, A.C.K., Poon, C.K.M. and Cheung, A.C.T. (2012) 'Effectiveness of facemasks to reduce exposure hazards for airborne infections among general populations.' *Journal of the Royal Society Interface*, 9(70), pp.938-948.

437. Leung, N.H., Chu, D.K., Shiu, E.Y., Chan, K.H., McDevitt, J.J., Hau, B.J., Yen, H.L., Li, Y., Ip, D.K., Peiris, J.M. and Seto, W.H. (2020) 'Respiratory virus shedding in exhaled breath and efficacy of face masks.' *Nature medicine*, 26(5), pp.676-680.

438. Guerra, D. and Guerra, D.J. (2021) 'Mask mandate and use efficacy in state-level COVID-19 containment', *medRxiv (Preprint)*.

439. Person, E., Lemercier, C., Royer, A. and Reychler, G. (2018) 'Effect of a surgical mask on six minute walking distance', *Revue des maladies respiratoires*, 35(3), pp.264-268.

440. Chandrasekaran, B. and Fernandes, S. 2020. '"Exercise with facemask; Are we handling a devil's sword?"–A physiological hypothesis', *Medical hypotheses*, 144(110002), pp.1-4.

441. Driver, S., Reynolds, M., Brown, K., Vingren, J.L., Hill, D.W., Bennett, M., Gilliland, T., McShan, E., Callender, L., Reynolds, E. and Borunda, N. 2021. 'Effects of wearing a cloth face mask on performance, physiological and perceptual responses during a graded treadmill running exercise test', *British journal of sports medicine, pp.1-7.*

442. Tong, P.S.Y., Kale, A.S., Ng, K., Loke, A.P., Choolani, M.A., Lim, C.L., Chan, Y.H., Chong, Y.S., Tambyah, P.A. and Yong, E.L. (2015) 'Respiratory consequences of N95-type Mask usage in pregnant healthcare workers - a controlled clinical study', *Antimicrobial Resistance & Infection Control*, 4(48), pp.1-10.

443. Kisielinski, K., Giboni, P., Prescher, A., Klosterhalfen, B., Graessel, D., Funken, S., Kempski, O. and Hirsch, O. (2021) 'Is a Mask That Covers the Mouth and Nose Free from Undesirable Side Effects in Everyday Use and Free of Potential Hazards?', *International journal of environmental research and public health*, 18(8), pp.1-42.

444. Morens, D.M., Taubenberger, J.K. and Fauci, A.S. (2008) 'Predominant Role of Bacterial Pneumonia as a Cause of Death in Pandemic Influenza: Implications for Pandemic Influenza Preparedness', *The Journal of infectious diseases,* 198(7), pp.962-970.

445. Parashar, Z. (2021) *Re-using a mask could cause 'Fungus', experts suggest these tips to avoid infection.* Available at: https://zeenews.india.com/india/black-fungus-is-use-of-unhygienic-masks-causing-the-infection-here-s-what-experts-believe-2363588.html (Accessed: 24 05 2021)

446. Chughtai, A.A., Stelzer-Braid, S., Rawlinson, W., Pontivivo, G., Wang, Q., Pan, Y., Zhang, D., Zhang, Y., Li, L. and MacIntyre, C.R. (2019) 'Contamination by respiratory viruses on outer surface of medical masks used by hospital healthcare workers', BMC infectious diseases, 19(1), pp.1-8.

447. Sullivan, G.L., Delgado-Gallardo, J., Watson, T.M. and Sarp, S. (2021) 'An investigation into the leaching of micro and nano particles and chemical pollutants from disposable face masks - linked to the COVID-19 pandemic', *Water Research*, 196(117033)

448. SAGE-Environmental Modelling Group (2021) EMG: Application of physical distancing and fabric face coverings in mitigating the B117 variant SARS-CoV-2 virus in public, workplace and community, 13 January 2021. Available at: https://www.gov.uk/government/publications/emg-application-of-physical-distancing-and-fabric-face-coverings-in-mitigating-the-b117-variant-sars-cov-2-virus-in-public-workplace-and-community (Accessed: 24 08 2021)

449. Office for Product Safety and Standards (2020) *Guidance for manufacturers and makers of face coverings to comply with the General Product Safety Regulations 2005: version 4.* Available at: https://assets.publishing.service.gov.uk/government/uploads/system/uploads/attachment_data/file/920648/Guidance-for-businesses-and-individuals-face-coverings-version-4.pdf (Accessed: 28 07 2021)

450. Han, J. and He, S. (2020) 'Need for assessing the inhalation of micro(nano)plastic debris shed from masks, respirators, and home-made face coverings during the COVID-19 pandemic.' *Environmental Pollution*, 268(115728), pp.1-4

451. Department of Health and Social Care (2021) Face coverings: when to wear one, exemptions, and how to make your own. Available at: https://www.gov.uk/government/publications/face-coverings-when-to-wear-one-and-how-to-make-your-own/face-coverings-when-to-wear-one-and-how-to-make-your-own?fbclid=IwAR1jdqY6x0GjLWXcbQT8XrTFwrp9eDegjqCA1KFHrUPIYtXZjaledtC7oFw (Accessed: 01 07 2021)

452. Howard, H. and Matthews, S. (2020) The calm, collected scientist leading UK's fight against coronavirus: New chief medical officer Professor Chris Whitty is a plague expert raised in Nigeria whose life was scarred as a teenager when his father was shot dead. Available at: https://www.dailymail.co.uk/health/article-8077813/Story-Chris-Whitty-Oxford-graduate-leading-Britains-fight-against-coronavirus.html (Accessed: 17 07 2021)

453. Wu, C. (2021) *Brisbane man 'suffers heart attack' after being arrested for not wearing a mask.* Available at: https://www.skynews.com.au/australia-news/coronavirus/brisbane-man-suffers-heart-attack-after-being-arrested-for-not-wearing-a-mask-while-exercising-in-lockdown/news-story/cc679efd8d27d7cbf5792eef75b6e857 (Accessed: 10 08 2021)

454. Loiacono, R. (2021) German Judge Declares Mask Mandates Illegal and Harmful to Children. Available at: https://www.theepochtimes.com/german-judge-declares-mask-mandates-illegal-and-harmful-to-children_3834457.html (Accessed: 02 06 2021)

455. Stoneman, J. (2021) *Cloth face masks are 'comfort blankets' that do little to curb Covid spread, Sage adviser warns.* Available at: https://www.telegraph.co.uk/news/2021/07/17/cloth-face-masks-comfort-blankets-do-little-curb-covid-spread/ (Accessed: 18 07 2021)

456. Centre for Health Security (2019) *About the Event 201 exercise.* Available at: https://www.centerforhealthsecurity.org/event201/about (Accessed: 23 04 2020)

457. Statista (2020) *Total number of all drug product recall enforcement reports issued by the FDA from 2012 to 2019.* Available at: https://www.statista.com/statistics/618383/total-fda-drug-enforcement-reports/ (Accessed: 10 01 2021)

458. Council of Europe (2021) *Covid-19 vaccines: ethical, legal, and practical considerations.* Available at: https://pace.coe.int/en/files/29004/html (Accessed: 20 06 2021)

459. Zhou, Y., Xu, J., Hou, Y., Leverenz, J.B., Kallianpur, A., Mehra, R., Liu, Y., Yu, H., Pieper, A.A., Jehi, L. and Cheng, F (2021) 'Network medicine links SARS-CoV-2/COVID19 infection to brain microvascular injury and neuroinflammation in dementia-like cognitive impairment.' *Alzheimer's Research & Therapy,* 13(10), pp.1-19.